Praise for *The Connection Code*

"As a mom and an athlete, I know how easy it is to lose yourself while taking care of everyone else. *The Connection Code* reminded me that taking care of my own alignment benefits not only myself but those around me. It's a win-win! Melissa has given women a powerful playbook for staying grounded, connected, and ready for whatever life throws at you."

— MIESHA TATE, former UFC Women's Bantamweight Champion, behavior change coach, and *Built for Growth* podcast host

"This book is a revolution wrapped in wisdom. Dr. Melissa doesn't just talk about connection—she embodies it, translating complex truths into practical, soulful action. *The Connection Code* is both a manual for remembering who we are and a map for how we heal individually and collectively. It's equal parts science, soul, and sovereignty."

— DR. NASHA WINTERS, ND, FABNO, author of *The Metabolic Approach to Cancer* and *Mistletoe and the Future of Integrative Oncology*

"No supplement or protocol can truly work if your nervous system is stuck in survival mode. That's why I love *The Connection Code* by Dr. Melissa Sonners. It's a powerful, science-backed approach to emotional healing and nervous system regulation that every woman needs, especially during the midlife shift. Dr. Melissa's work bridges the science of the nervous system with the soul of human connection, offering practical, powerful tools that help you feel safe, grounded, and truly present in your life again. This is the missing piece we've been waiting for."

— DR. MARIZA SNYDER, best-selling author of *The Perimenopause Revolution* and host of *Energized* podcast

"This book is a reminder that the answers we're searching for aren't out there, they're inside us. Melissa shows us how to quiet the noise, tune in to the wisdom of the body, and reconnect with the whole self. Reading *The Connection Code* feels like being guided home."

— KHALIL RAFATI, founder and owner of SunLife Organics, best-selling author of *I Forgot to Die,* and speaker and entrepreneur

"As a lymphatic expert, I know firsthand that true healing (and drainage) doesn't happen if your nervous system is stuck in survival mode. That's why *The Connection Code* is so powerful. Melissa gives women the tools to shift into safety and alignment, so the body can finally do what it was designed to do: rest, repair, and thrive. This book is a must-read for anyone ready to stop fighting their body and start flowing with it."
— **Dr. Caitlin Czezowski (aka Doc.Talks.Detox)**, DC, CFMP, CACCP

"Connection is everything, especially for women! You know I'm a big fan of oxytocin, and real connection is one of the best ways to boost it. In *The Connection Code*, Melissa Sonners captures the true essence of connection in such a beautiful and relatable way. She speaks straight to the heart of her readers, reminding us that true healing is possible. This is a must-read for anyone craving deeper bonds and more joy."
— **Dr. Anna Cabeca**, The Girlfriend Doctor; triple board-certified gynecologist and obstetrician; board-certified in Integrative Medicine, Anti-Aging, and Regenerative Medicine; best-selling author of *The Hormone Fix*

"*The Connection Code* is a beautifully grounded, science-meets-spirit guide to creating a life that feels every bit as good, if not better than it looks. For anyone who senses there's more aliveness, depth, or expression waiting to be unlocked, this book is a truly transformative companion."
— **Kate Northrup**, best-selling author of *Do Less*

"Dr. Melissa Sonners reveals one of the greatest longevity secrets of all, genuine connection. *The Connection Code* reminds us that healing and vitality don't just come from what we eat or how we move, but from the communities that help us feel seen, supported, and aligned."
— **Ben Azadi**, *New York Times* best-selling author of *Metabolic Freedom*

"Sleep isn't just something that happens at night, it's the result of how safe and connected you feel during the day. *The Connection Code* reminds us that rest begins with regulation. With approachable, two-minute practices and science-backed winsight, Dr. Sonners helps women create rhythms that quiet the mind, calm the body, and bring peace of mind back to bedtime."
 — **MOLLIE EASTMAN**, sleep expert and founder of Sleep Is a Skill, host of the *Sleep Is a Skill* podcast

"Melissa beautifully bridges what I love most: science and soul. She teaches that regulation isn't just a nervous system process; it's a remembrance of who we are beneath the noise and conditioning. *The Connection Code* is a guide for every woman ready to stop fixing herself and start feeling herself again. Melissa provides a simple and practical framework along with daily practices to help women heal and transform. Giving women permission to live a vital life filled with connection and joy."
 — **DR. SONYA JENSEN, ND**, author of *Heal Your Hormones, Reclaim Yourself*

"*The Connection Code* is equal parts science, soul, and 'oh wow, that's me.' Dr. Sonners has a rare gift of turning complex psychology into something that feels like a conversation with a friend who truly sees you. The book will leave you feeling clearer, lighter, and connected with your life in a whole new way."
 — **CASE KENNY**, optimism expert, author, and keynote speaker

"*The Connection Code* cuts through the noise. Melissa shows you that your system isn't broken—it's overloaded—and she gives you the tools to reset it. If you want to feel grounded, clear, and capable again, start here."
 — **MIKE R. HOLLAND**, creator of the Mind Body Energy Movement

Hay House Titles of Related Interest

YOU CAN HEAL YOUR LIFE, the movie,
starring Louise Hay & Friends
(available as an online streaming video)
www.hayhouse.co.uk/louise-movie

THE SHIFT, the movie,
starring Dr Wayne W. Dyer
(available as an online streaming video)
www.hayhouse.co.uk/the-shift-movie

✱ ✱ ✱

AGE LIKE A GIRL: How Menopause Rewires Your Brain for Mental Clarity, Increased Confidence and Renewed Energy, by Dr Mindy Pelz

BREAKING THE HABIT OF BEING YOURSELF: How to Lose Your Mind and Create a New One, by Dr Joe Dispenza

DO LESS: A Revolutionary Approach to Time and Energy Management for Ambitious Women, by Kate Northrup

THE LET THEM THEORY: A Life-Changing Tool That Millions of People Can't Stop Talking About, by Mel Robbins

SELF HELP: This Is Your Chance to Change Your Life, by Gabrielle Bernstein

All of the above are available at your local bookstore,
or may be ordered by visiting:

Hay House UK: www.hayhouse.co.uk
Hay House USA: www.hayhouse.com®
Hay House Australia: www.hayhouse.com.au
Hay House India: www.hayhouse.co.in

The Connection Code

Unlock the Secrets to Realignment with Your Truest Self

DR MELISSA SONNERS

HAY HOUSE

Carlsbad, California • New York City
London • Sydney • New Delhi

Published in the United Kingdom by:
Hay House UK Ltd, 1st Floor, Crawford Corner,
91–93 Baker Street, London W1U 6QQ
Tel: +44 (0)20 3927 7290; www.hayhouse.co.uk

Text © Dr Melissa Sonners, 2026

The moral rights of the author have been asserted.

All rights reserved. No part of this book may be reproduced by any mechanical, photographic or electronic process, or in the form of a phonographic recording; nor may it be stored in a retrieval system, transmitted or otherwise be copied for public or private use, other than for 'fair use' as brief quotations embodied in articles and reviews, without prior written permission of the publisher.

The information given in this book should not be treated as a substitute for professional medical advice; always consult a medical practitioner. Any use of information in this book is at the reader's discretion and risk. Neither the author nor the publisher can be held responsible for any loss, claim or damage arising out of the use, or misuse, of the suggestions made, the failure to take medical advice or for any material on third-party websites.

A catalogue record for this book is available from the British Library.

Tradepaper ISBN: 978-1-83782-514-1
E-book ISBN: 978-1-4019-9791-5
Audiobook ISBN: 978-1-4019-9792-2

10 9 8 7 6 5 4 3 2 1

This product uses responsibly sourced papers, including recycled materials and materials from other controlled sources.
For more information, see www.hayhouse.co.uk

The authorized representative in the EU for product safety and compliance is Penguin Random House Ireland, Morrison Chambers, 32 Nassau Street, Dublin D02 YH68, Ireland. https://eu-contact.penguin.ie

Printed and bound by CPI Group (UK) Ltd, Croydon CR0 4YY

To you.
The one holding this book.
Maybe you picked it up out of curiosity.
Maybe you're hoping this "code" will help you feel different.
Maybe somewhere along the way, you lost pieces of yourself to career, to motherhood, to keeping everyone else whole.
I want you to know this: You are not lost.
You don't need to become anything more.
Everything you've been searching for is already within you.
This isn't a path of striving; it's a path of remembering.
Let this be your gentle reminder that your light never left, it's simply waiting for you to return.
Welcome home.

To Jason. My dreamboy.
Thank you for being the partner who held our family, our businesses, and every moving piece so I could bring this vision to life. Thank you for loving every version of me and for standing steady as I peeled back the layers of who I became while raising kids and building a career and found my way back to the girl you fell in love with: the fun, whimsical, Midwest-hearted girl who moved through the world in her own rhythm long before she had language for alignment.

To Levi, Wyatt, and Kaia.
You are my greatest creation and the coolest kids I know. You are also my daily accountability to live what I teach. Thank you for giving me a million reasons to do the work so that I can stay present for all the moments that truly matter.

CONTENTS

Foreword xi
Introduction xiii

PART 1: MISALIGNMENTS 1
Chapter 1: The Science of Disconnection 3
Chapter 2: Meet Your Ego: Your Overprotective Big Sister 16
Chapter 3: The Myths of Womanhood 32
Chapter 4: Be. Do. Have. 46
Chapter 5: Breaking Free. 59

PART 2: GETTING ALIGNED 67
Chapter 6: Teaming Up with Your Ego 69
Chapter 7: Gifts of the Ego 82
Chapter 8: The Connection Code. 96
Chapter 9: Creating Community 112
Chapter 10: Coming Home: Ancestral Wisdom & Alignment. 126

PART 3: STAYING ALIGNED. 153
Chapter 11: Holding Alignment. 155
Chapter 12: It's Not Selfish, It's Self-WITH 168
Chapter 13: Creating Inner Beacons. 180
Chapter 14: The Path to You: A Road Map for Realignment 192

Conclusion 203
Resources 210
Endnotes 211
Acknowledgments 213
About the Author 219

FOREWORD

There are certain people who walk into your life and instantly change the atmosphere. Dr. Melissa Sonners is one of those people. Her presence carries both the science and the soul of healing—a rare combination that reminds you that transformation doesn't come from trying harder, it comes from returning home to yourself.

I've watched Melissa live and breathe the very principles you're about to discover in *The Connection Code*. I've seen her navigate life's hardest moments: motherhood, business, illness, reinvention, with a grace that only comes from deep inner alignment. What she's offering here is not theory. It's lived wisdom.

We live in a world that's louder than ever—more notifications, more noise, more expectations pulling us away from our center. And for women especially, this disconnection becomes an invisible weight. We start to believe that exhaustion is normal, that busyness equals worth, that stillness is indulgent. Melissa's words are the antidote to that cultural lie. She reminds us that we are not broken; we're just misaligned. And that real healing begins not in doing more, but in listening more deeply.

What I love about *The Connection Code* is that it gives women permission to slow down and reconnect. Melissa bridges neuroscience, energy work, and feminine wisdom in a way that feels both scientific and sacred. You'll find practical tools here, but also a deeper invitation: to meet yourself again with compassion and curiosity.

In my own work with women around the world, I've seen that true health doesn't start with a new diet or a longer fast—it starts with connection. Connection to your body, your intuition, your community, and something greater than yourself. This book is a road map back to that connection. It's the missing link so many of us have been searching for.

If you've been feeling lost, overextended, or like you're constantly giving pieces of yourself away, this book will feel like a deep exhale. Melissa will guide you gently, like the wise, grounded friend who's walked the path before you, showing you how to come home to your own rhythm again.

As you turn these pages, my hope is that you allow yourself to be seen in her words. To see your story reflected back not as something to fix, but as something sacred to understand. Because when you reconnect with your true self, you don't just heal . . . you realign with the life that was always meant for you.

With deep admiration,

Dr. Mindy Pelz, DC

New York Times best-selling author of *Fast Like a Girl, Eat Like a Girl,* and *Age Like a Girl*

INTRODUCTION

You feel it, don't you?

There is a quiet pain inside of you; something is missing but you can't quite figure out what. On the outside, everything looks fine. You are showing up as the best person you can possibly be. You tick off the to-do list, meet the deadlines, have meals on the table, do your best to ensure your family's health and happiness, and keep yourself together. Everything might even be picture-perfect and ready to share on social media. The talking points of your life are all in order; at social gatherings everyone says, "Wow! I don't know how you do it!"

But on the inside, things don't feel so good.

There is a pull you have felt for a while, and it's getting harder to ignore. Dissatisfaction is seeping into your life, and it makes itself apparent in surprising ways. Even when you are with people, you feel lonely. The relationships you have feel a little hollow, even superficial. You don't get alone time . . . and if you do, you don't know what to do with it. You might even avoid it since you're not being productive in those moments and that undermines the constant race toward perfection that you signed up for at some point . . . although you don't remember when, or that you even agreed to be a participant. You crave peace, but stolen moments of relaxation feel selfish. You might even hear a little voice in your head accusing you of letting others down the moment that you take time for yourself.

It's safer to ignore those feelings, stick with the life you've created. It's safer to *blend in*. You've been doing what you believe you're supposed to do—sacrificing your own well-being—for so long that you've forgotten what it feels like to *stand in* who you truly are. That center of resilience, that internal force from your childhood and youth, the light within that drove you, is still there—and it's waiting for you to come home and reconnect with your whole self.

THE UNSPOKEN TRUTH OF BLENDING IN

The need to blend in isn't something you chose, it's something you were taught. From a young age you were conditioned to be good, nice, not make a scene, not cause a problem, not speak up because it might cause conflict. As a child, you learned early on that your role in the world was as a peacemaker and an uncomplaining, unpaid laborer—both of which benefit other people, not you. As an adult, you've been praised for being agreeable, easygoing, and kind. That's worked for a while, it's made people like you, it's kept you from being judged, criticized, outcasted, or called "too much." Society has rewarded you for fitting into the mold of the devoted partner, nurturing mother, loyal friend, and accommodating co-worker.

But there is a cost.

Blending in causes us to disconnect from some of the most beautiful, essential pieces of ourselves. The parts that make us unique, that are aligned with our life's purpose and calling. Piece by piece you have tucked away your opinions, your quirks, your truth. You have dulled your edges so as not to upset, disappoint, or lose anyone.

INTRODUCTION

But in doing so you have disappointed and lost yourself.

If these words are resonating with you, I want you to know you are not broken. You are not alone. I have been there—and I found a way out. When my children were ages six, four, and one, I was diagnosed with meningitis and encephalitis due to neurological Lyme disease combined with mold toxicity. At that point in my life, I was doing it all. I was working full-time as a chiropractor, leading a wonderful life with my husband, raising three children, keeping the house clean, working out, and checking all the boxes. My life was as put-together as it could possibly be. Everything was perfect—except, of course, it wasn't. I had built a castle with no foundation; I had set up a lifestyle that was not sustainable without investing in myself.

Because of that stressed and cracked base, a single bite from a tick and some spores floating in the air brought my world to a crashing halt. I literally lost my mind. I would forget my kids' names. I couldn't find my way to work—two miles away in an office my husband and I had built together, and I'd been working in for 15 years. The recovery was frustrating and debilitating. I felt as if I was causing disruption in my family as my role shifted from caretaker to being taken care of. But it was also clarifying; it made me take a hard look at how I'd been living my life, and how worn down I was. Once I was physically better, I knew I couldn't return to my old ways. I couldn't go back to blending in and doing what I felt I was supposed to do. In order to be a healthy, whole woman, I had to stop self-sacrificing. I had to stand in myself.

That meant self-care, but the traditional methods of self-care that are built into our society—manicures, massages, pedicures—only feel great in the moment. They don't have lasting effects. In a moment of stress a week later, can you look back at that manicure and still draw comfort and peace from it? No, you can't. That's because so many of our modern self-care practices focus on *doing* instead of *being*. That manicure, massage, or pedicure was for the length of an appointment, and the results faded away.

At the end of a long day, when for whatever reason you still need to keep going—whether it's to now prepare dinner for your family, or grab groceries, or call that friend who has been needing to talk—are you actually able to access the traditional tools/model of self-care? I mean, if we could just turn off all the responsibilities and lie on a massage table, that alone would feel amazing! But the reality is, there are many real-life moments where we need a little something-something to help us feel better in real time. In the actual moment when your co-worker triggers you and you're trying to get composed while in a meeting with all eyes on you, or when your mother-in-law yet again throws your values and wishes under the table and you feel disrespected, but it's not the appropriate time or you're not in the energy you actually want to be in to have that convo. Or you're running out the door late, you spill your coffee on your white shirt, then hit traffic, someone cuts you off, and your day is just feeling horrible from the get-go, and you want to do something to make it better.

But taking the rest of the day off to go to the spa isn't in your reality. What do you do in these moments? This is where I had to learn to flip the model that I knew of for self-care on its head. When I practiced self-care, what I was really doing was connecting to myself. It reminded me that what all those self-care tools do is help us get out of our busy heads and drop all the layers of stress so we can come back home to our bodies. They remind us to breathe again and connect us to ourselves. What if there was a way to access that feeling

INTRODUCTION

and result in real time? That was the question I aimed to answer. And what I discovered was that coming home to ourselves again isn't a to-do item (audibly exhale—one less item on our never-ending to-do list). Rather, it's a simple shift in focus on who we BE, and that changes everything. It reminds us that WE can be our own anchor, a steady and calm place. We've been taught to look out there for the reset, the fix, the appointment that will finally bring us back home and help us feel like ourselves again. But what if the answer doesn't come through something you schedule but something you remember?

Instead of quick fixes and escapes from our lives, we're instead creating a new way. We're flipping the model on self-care. We're discovering the truth—we're not broken, just misaligned. This is a practice of presence of awareness and choosing differently. It's not an appointment or a supplement, it's a shift in who you can BE. This new way doesn't fade when the massage is over and you drop back into your life. It's lasting, it's embodied, it's aligned, and it's yours. Learning how to reconnect with your true self is a practice of *being*, one that you can return to at any time, as often as you want, when you need to be refreshed. True self-care and connection are not about carving out time for appointments; they're about fostering and nurturing an inner relationship so that you can stay grounded and aligned—even when the sign at the salon is turned to CLOSED.

Before I got sick, I remember many moments at the end of a long day, hearing a little whisper that I couldn't do it, or I needed rest, or that I needed something for me, but in my mind, it wasn't an option. I couldn't go get a massage; I needed to cook dinner. I wasn't able to sneak out for an appointment the moment I finally got done with work; I needed to get home to my kids. So instead of listening to that voice, I drowned it out in a glass of wine so I could feel like I was actually doing something for me.

Now, in hindsight I realize that THESE new tools of CONNECTION are the true self-care that is needed AND accessible to today's woman. In that moment when I was cooking dinner and needing something for me, I could have paused, asked myself what it was that I needed, listened, and given myself some tiny version of that. Need a rest? Perhaps I could promise myself a nice bath afterward. Need more joy? Perhaps I could have blasted the music and rocked out while I cooked. Although seemingly subtle, these practices that allow us to tune in, listen to our selves again, and take tiny steps to feed our souls are the ones that make the greatest impacts.

WHAT THIS BOOK CAN DO FOR YOU

You are ready for something different, and that's exactly what you're about to get. You're ready to feel like you again. This book is your guide back to yourself. Here is what you can expect.

Awareness: How often have you achieved something, or found a moment of peace, only to have a little voice in your head speak up and tell you that it's not enough, that the other shoe will drop soon, or that even though you managed everything today, you're still an impostor? Do you have a nagging feeling that you're not doing life as well as the ultra-mom next door, who gets everything done and still looks amazing? You will soon discover the hidden messages your ego has been trying to tell you. These often feel like triggers, upset, or stress. Beneath all that is a powerful message that will help guide you back to yourself, allowing you to show up as a whole person—not just the female cardboard cutout that society has molded you into.

Connection: You'll learn how to reconnect with yourself at any moment. This will no longer require checking out of your life for a one-hour appointment. You will be able to establish connection in the micro-moments during your commute, while running a carpool, before going into a work meeting, and even when your child is having a meltdown at the worst possible moment.

Alignment: With the help of the prompts, resources, and tools shared here, you will build your very own personalized connection kit. This is a set of tools that is easy to implement at the moment and can be used in almost any situation. Over a short time, these will become second nature to who you are. Restoring yourself back to calm and centered amid chaos will become just what you do.

HOW THIS BOOK IS ORGANIZED

This book is structured into three parts. In Part 1: Misalignments, you'll learn about why this has happened to you in the first place. How many times have you tried a new program, set a new goal, or made a New Year's resolution, only to fall back into your old habits? This happens because many trends in shaping a new you don't first explain *why* you are the way you are. In order to move on, you must first understand how you arrived here. The first section of this book will help you understand the powerful forces at work—both inside and outside of you—that have kept you stuck for all these years.

In Part 2: Getting Aligned, you will learn how to implement real, lasting changes in your life based on a methodology that I developed for myself, and that has gotten me back to my whole self—the version of me that stands in rather than blends in. The second part of the book is designed to help you utilize real-world, actionable, and practical steps to reconnect with your whole self—the version that has been waiting for you to return to it, waiting for you to come back home to yourself.

The third section of the book, Part 3: Staying Aligned, is critical in reminding you that change isn't easy and it doesn't happen overnight. You will backslide. You will have rough moments and bad days. You will find yourself relying on old habits and comforts that kept you stuck—but that's okay! Just because you fall out of alignment with your true self doesn't mean you can't get back to good. This concluding section of the book will help you navigate those times when you feel like you're not moving forward and will show you how to get back on the right path.

By the end, you'll know how to approach life as your whole self. You'll stop feeling the need to dim your inner light in order to make others more comfortable. You'll stop muting your voice in order to keep the peace, and you'll finally come home to your true self.

You are not broken for feeling lost. You are not the only woman feeling disconnected. You are not selfish for craving something more. This isn't a flaw; it's a signal. That pain you feel is your whole self calling you back home.

It's time to stop blending in and start standing in your power.

Let's begin.

Part 1

MISALIGNMENTS

CHAPTER 1

The Science of Disconnection

Why do we stay stuck?

It's something that all of us have wrestled with at one point or another; you are not alone when you look at where you are and perhaps feel a deep sense of dissatisfaction. It's human nature to want to grow, evolve, level up, and go for more. Unfortunately, you're also not alone if you've turned away from that feeling because the thought of upending your life, or making big changes is just . . . too scary. Why do we stay in relationships that drain us, be they romantic, friendship circles, or in the workplace? Why do we stay in jobs that we hate, or continue to play small and blend in, even when it's crushing our spirit?

Here's the answer—it's not because there's something wrong with you. You've berated yourself before, called yourself lazy, weak, or a coward. But the truth is that you are none of these things. You aren't simply settling for less or confusing contentment with stagnation. The truth is that your brain is hardwired to keep you where you are, because your brain craves familiarity more than it craves happiness. It can be a hard concept to process, but your own brain is working against you—even though it thinks it's helping!

YOUR BRAIN & ITS LOVE AFFAIR WITH FAMILIARITY

To fully grasp why you stay stuck, we need to understand a key component in the brain—your amygdala. The amygdala is a small, almond-shaped part of the brain that plays a mighty role in keeping you safe by detecting threats and activating your fight-or-flight response. This mechanism kept our ancestors alive—and ensured that our species endured—back when hunting for food could also mean that you were being stalked by a tiger. Have you ever seen movement out of the corner of your eye that made you flinch or jumped when something unexpected happened? Your heart races, your body is flooded with cortisol and adrenaline. You might even get black spots in your vision because your brain redirects a large amount of blood to your legs so that you can run.

That's your amygdala kicking in, alerting you to danger and making split-second decisions about which trauma response will suit you best in the moment—fight (physically defend your body) or flight (flee from the scene). Our amygdala operates on a hair trigger and doesn't distinguish between real and imagined threats, which is why you have the same reaction to your spouse unexpectedly coming up behind you as you do to the fire alarm going off at work. The amygdala did a wonderful job of protecting our ancestors from predators, rockslides, and other humans, and we're all here today as a result. However, it's still operating at the same somewhat panicky rate in a world where we are much safer.

As a result, the amygdala is still searching for threats—whether they warrant a stress reaction or not. Today, you don't have to worry about being chased by a tiger, but your mother-in-law might have taken its place. The driver in front of you who is looking at their phone and doesn't notice when the light turns green isn't an actual threat to you, but they might make you late for work—a version of danger in the modern world. So your amygdala reacts accordingly and pumps out all the chemicals your body needs to perform fight-or-flight, whether the cause is your kid having a meltdown in the back seat or your triggering co-worker hijacking the peace and quiet of your lunch break.

Our jungle today is a concrete one, but it's still the wild, where uncertainty equals danger. Your nervous system hasn't evolved enough to tell the difference between being chased by a lion and being interviewed for a new job. Physiologically, your brain and body react in the same way. The amygdala is constantly scanning your environment for threats, and it doesn't care whether they're physical, emotional, or mental. It will wear you out if you let it, because this ancient, powerful section of your brain doesn't care if you're happy—it only cares if you're safe.

To the amygdala, familiar things are safe. This is why routines play a calming role in our lives. Do you have a favorite side of the bed? Always drive the same route to work? Is there a coffee shop you always stop at in the morning or a lunch spot that is a must? Do you feel a sense of discomfort when you go into a new restaurant and have to contend with an unfamiliar menu? How about walking into a new fitness class where you don't know anyone, aren't sure which locker you should use, or suddenly realize that everyone else is wearing leggings and you have on shorts?

Routines, familiar places, and consistency are ways that your amygdala helps control your environment so that you feel safe. This is why we cling to old patterns and situations, even when we know they are actually bad for us. Toxic relationships, exhausting work environments, and sabotaging habits are all painful, but they are also predictable. In this way, even a mediocre romantic relationship can bring comfort simply because your brain processes the idea of being alone—or dating again—as too scary an alternative.

According to Dr. Joe Dispenza, *New York Times* best-selling author and an expert on epigenetics and neuroscience, our brains prioritize what is familiar not only because it's less frightening, but it's also easier and energy efficient.[1]

According to *Psychology Today*, familiar situations and environments require less mental effort to process. This ease of processing is known as "perceptual fluency," and it makes familiar experiences more appealing because they conserve cognitive resources and are easier for the brain to handle, even if they keep us feeling stuck or falling into old behaviors, patterns, or circles that no longer serve us. A familiar hell feels "safer" than an unknown potential heaven.[2]

Old patterns require less thought than creating new ones. Think about your daily commute. How often have you arrived at work and can't even remember driving there? That's your brain zoning out, drifting, daydreaming, or planning your day as you were driving because it knows the route so well that you don't have to be fully present to navigate it.

Contrast this to driving while on vacation or in an unfamiliar place. You've got Google Maps up on your phone, you're sitting forward in your seat, both hands on the wheel, reading street signs and constantly checking your mirrors because you might have to make a sudden lane change. Any tendency you had toward frustration with other drivers is now magnified by 20—every car that cuts you off is identified as an enemy, every person behind the wheel who wouldn't let you into the exit lane is someone you will hold a personal grudge against for the rest of the day, if not longer. You're sweaty and shaking, ready to fight in order to get to your destination.

Any time you attempt something new—like standing in your truth rather than safely blending in—your amygdala gets triggered. Your brain literally tells you that what you are doing is different, and different can be dangerous. This is why you stay stuck in habits, patterns, relationships, careers, and friendships circles that no longer serve you—not because you are cowardly, weak, or lazy. Staying stuck isn't your fault; it's your biology. Understanding this will help you have more compassion for yourself and help you fully understand why making positive changes in the past has been so difficult.

The Power of the Comfort Zone

We often hear about the power of stepping out of your comfort zone, but let's be real—staying in the comfort zone feels good because it's easy and predictable. Your comfort zone is any physical, emotional, or mental space where you feel you have a sense of control—even if that ability to control it comes at the expense of your growth, joy, or fulfillment. The comfort zone can feel like security, but it's really just familiar suffering wrapped up with a pretty ribbon to keep you stuck.

There are a few reasons why we choose familiar pain over unknown possibility. Your amygdala is once again the prime culprit. If you've survived an experience, your amygdala files it away as something that you can endure and will live through if it happens again. Having a boyfriend who neglects you emotionally doesn't feel good, but who is to say the next guy won't be worse? You've survived being neglected, and you can read his signals now, maybe even predict when things are going to take a downswing. Your brain will continue to choose known pain over unknown possibility; rather than break up with him in the hopes of finding someone better, you stay in the relationship out of fear of ending up with someone worse.

It might be hard to believe, but you can also become addicted to stress. The stress hormones of adrenaline and cortisol that your brain pumps into your system put you on high alert and add an edge to your awareness. Living under constant stress can lead you to a point where experiencing a moment of calm can actually leave you feeling ungrounded and unanchored. Ever had an evening to yourself, but you use it to check work e-mails? Ever sat down with your morning coffee and made your to-do list at the same time, even though you could absolutely do that later?

Lastly, you stay in your comfort zone because your brain hates contradictions. That little voice that tells you that you're not worthy or aren't enough *wants* to be right, so your brain will seek out situations, relationships, and conditions that prove it to be true. This all happens subconsciously and is called *confirmation bias*. Your brain searches for proof that what it believes—and has been conditioned to believe since childhood—is correct and often discards evidence to the contrary. This is why so many stay in environments that no longer serve them. Your brain chases familiarity, not freedom.

Now that you know all this, hopefully you realize that past failed attempts at breaking out of cycles aren't your fault. You can finally stop beating yourself up, but guess what? There's even more good news. Your brain can change. You can teach, rewire, and retrain your brain that uncertainty is welcome, change is good, and the bake sale you didn't know about but is happening tomorrow is not a threat. And that's exactly what we're going to do together in this book!

Every time you lean into the unknown, you are teaching your brain. Every time you get to the other side of a new experience, your brain recognizes the better options that await you. A new path forms in your brain, making it easier to make the decision for change the next time. That doesn't mean it will always be a smooth path; you'll still experience fear of the unknown from time to time, but as you slowly expose your brain to the benefits of breaking cycles, your negative reactions will become less powerful.

The beginning of carving a new path is the hardest, but it will continue to get easier and easier over time. You are teaching your brain that uncertainty isn't something to solve your way out of by resorting to old patterns. It's something you can face together. You are going to learn to partner with yourself and team up with gentle compassion. Your new mantra: Uncertainty isn't a threat—it's an invitation to grow.

The Dopamine Reward System

Another reason why it can be so difficult to break out of your old cycles is because of dopamine, a naturally occurring pleasure chemical. Your brain releases dopamine as a reward; that warm, fuzzy feeling in your tummy when you do something nice for someone, or that spike of affection you feel when you lock eyes with your significant other? That's dopamine at work. Dopamine is involved in everything you do that makes you feel good, from eating food to having sex to petting your dog.

But dopamine can also lead you astray. As functioning adults, we know that not everything that *feels* good is necessarily good *for* you. The feeling of happiness that comes from eating a good meal quickly takes a darker tone if that meal was an entire box of Little Debbie's. Sex without emotional connection may feel good in the moment but will leave you feeling empty afterward. In fact, dopamine plays a large role in addiction. Opioids deliver an unnatural amount of dopamine to the brain, bringing a sense of euphoria that cannot be rivaled by everyday things. Even if you think you have healthy boundaries in your life around things like sex, drugs, or food, dopamine is a factor in your habits and one of the tools your brain uses to keep you stuck.

Comfort is a form of pleasure, and we return to the things that make us feel good because of the dopamine hit our brain gets. Even innocuous acts like scrolling through your phone cause a dopamine release in your brain. Dr. Anna Lembke, a world-leading expert on addiction, calls the smartphone the "modern-day hypodermic needle."[3] Since smartphones were introduced in our culture, behavioral addiction (things you do) rather than substance addiction (things you consume) has soared. If reaching for your phone is how you detox from the day, consider the possibility that it might be having the completely opposite effect.

Your brain wants dopamine and will do just about anything to get it. This is another reason why breaking away from those old habits is so difficult; it literally feels like you're being rewarded when you indulge in them. Luckily, lots of things in life can feel good, and you can retrain your brain to recognize new and different things as pleasurable, helping to establish new patterns that will encourage you to stand in rather than blend in.

THE SCIENCE OF DISCONNECTION

REFLECTIVE PROMPTS

1. Goal: Identify Your Comfort Zone:
- What is one area of your life, whether it be relationships, career, self-care, habits, etc., where you feel stuck or unsatisfied?
- What is it about this situation that feels familiar or safe, even though it's no longer serving you?

2. Examine the Trade-Offs:
- What are the real or perceived benefits of staying in this pattern or situation?
- What is it costing you to stay here?

3. Uncover the Fears:
- What are you afraid might happen if you step out of this pattern and attempt something new?
- What is the worst-case scenario?
- How likely is that to happen?

4. Imagine a New Way:
- Visualize yourself in the new situation you have created once you let go of the old way. What does your life look and feel like now?
- What could you gain by letting go of this old pattern?

5. Notice What Shows Up:
- When or where does this old pattern show up most?
- Are there certain people or situations that bring it out?

Exercises

1. Pattern Spotting Chart:

Old Pattern	Pattern 1	Pattern 2	Pattern 3
Why it feels safe			
What it's costing me			
How would it feel to release it			

2. Stretch Your Comfort Zone:

- Choose one small action that pulls you out of this old pattern. Maybe it's speaking up when you disagree, saying no to something you feel obligated to do, or trying something new.
- Put this into action for one day and journal about how it goes. How do you feel while doing it? How do you feel after? Continue to flex this muscle and practice your new habit. It will continue to get easier and more natural.

3. Dialogue That Voice Keeping You Stuck:

- Write a letter in your journal to the voice as if it were a person. Ask it what it's afraid of and write out the response.

4. Role-Play:

- It can be easier to help guide our friends through a challenge than it is to see a way out of our own. Create some distance from you and your challenge by pretending it's your friend stuck in this situation. How would you help her through? What advice would you give her? Ask yourself, why is it difficult for you to follow that advice?

5. Comfort Zone Mapping:

- Draw a circle on the page and label it Comfort Zone. Inside, list all the habits, situations, and relationships that are familiar but limiting.
- Outside the circle write down anything you want to try out as you grow but haven't felt safe doing so yet.
- Reflect on active steps you can take each day to bridge the gap between the inner and outer circle.

6. Affirmations:

Print these out and stick them to your bathroom mirror or add them to your phone or computer screensaver so you will see them often:

- I am safe to grow, change, and explore new possibilities.
- I am making the uncomfortable comfortable.
- I trust what is on the other side of this.
- I choose what aligns with the future I am creating for myself.

7. Name It to Tame It:

Naming the uncertainty helps make the subjective objective. That indefinable feeling of dissatisfaction or fear can be addressed once you know exactly what it is that you are fearful of when uncertainty arises.

- If you are scrolling through your phone rather than starting that new work project, ask yourself why. Is it because you are afraid you will fail?
- If you are in conflict with a loved one but choose not to address it, is it because you are afraid you will lose them?

- Create an awareness of yourself when you reach for what's familiar or comfortable in times of uncertainty; it's the first and most powerful step in breaking this pattern.

8. Soothe the Amygdala:

I like to visualize my amygdala as a frightened child, and my job is to soothe her. Rather than letting her overreact to a perceived threat, I take charge as the parent and remind her we are safe.

- Use a five-minute grounding tool like breathwork, a grounding pulsed electromagnetic field mat—a cushioned mat that sends gentle, magnetic pulses through your body to recharge your cells, boost blood flow, and support restoration—a nature walk, laughing, or anything else you enjoy outside of the digital world. This tells your amygdala that you are safe, despite its initial reaction.

- When you feel safe, your prefrontal cortex—the logical part of the brain—will come back online, making it easier for you to think clearly and rationally.

9. Rewrite the Pattern:

Remember, your old patterns are familiar, even if they are illogical and not necessarily good for you. If you feel yourself slipping back into old patterns, simply recognizing that you are doing so is the first step toward change.

- The next time you feel yourself falling back into a comfort zone, try saying something silly to yourself aloud. "Ha! I see you sneaking up on me, old patterns."

- This will signal to your brain that we're trying something new; it's the beginning of rewiring your brain.

10. Create Dopamine Micro-Wins:

If dopamine is really good at keeping you stuck, let's retrain it and use its powers to help you move forward. Small wins can also trigger dopamine and create a feel-good reward moment for your brain and body.

- Every time you take a step toward a new habit for five minutes—like hitting up a nature walk and actually being present in those moments or rethinking it when you automatically reach for your phone—you're wiring a tiny win. Each one gives your brain a dose of dopamine, reinforcing the new behavior and making it feel more natural and effortless next time.

- Chunk your big goals into smaller, more tangible steps. Aim for five minutes of something good, rather than an hour. In this way, you can retrain your brain so that it learns healthy new habits can *also* feel good. Microdose your new life!

CHAPTER 2

Meet Your Ego: Your Overprotective Big Sister

There is another force at play in staying small—your ego. If you have ever heard that voice inside your head narrating your life, your every move, overanalyzing every conversation and situation, or second-guessing your choices anytime you wear something a little too bold—congrats, you've met her.

That's your ego.

Contrary to popular opinion and what we've been taught about the ego, she isn't the villain in your life. Rather, she is a person—and she's a bit *extra*. She's a misguided big sister figure who thinks she knows best and simply aims to protect you. She's type A, perhaps wound a little too tight, maybe a bit anxious. She's got a clipboard in hand with an annotated version of your life and is always ready to provide an unsolicited opinion. She's a master at dictating how you show up in the world. And like most overprotective big sister figures, her tactics are a bit intense. She wasn't always so overbearing, and that clipboard she uses to record all your past experiences didn't always have so many notes on it. She was *taught* and *conditioned* to show up this way by society.

Your ego was born when you were a little girl. She grew with you, always keeping a tight focus on your behavior and choices as she learned how to navigate the world. At first—like you—she was playful and free-spirited. Curious, wide-eyed, and just wanted to move through the world by both giving *and* receiving love. But then something happened, and it changed her. It might have occurred when someone laughed at your haircut or when a teacher criticized you in front of the whole class. It might have been that singular painful moment when you fully expressed your wild-hearted self, your dreams and ambitions, your wants and desires, only to be shut down. Only to be told you were thinking too big.

That's when your protective big sister ego figure stepped in. She felt what happened, got back up from the ground—because make no mistake, this was a blow—dusted herself off, and made a decision that would impact the rest of your life. She realized that the world can be a harsh place and that the people in it were not always on your side. In fact, some might be actively working against you. Going forward she would aim to protect you, to never let you feel shunned or too much or different again.

She took careful notes every time you felt embarrassed, rejected, or vulnerable. She watched for reactions and assumed any scowl, stare, or hushed whispers meant you were doing something wrong. She studied the patterns, and with each experience that felt a little bit off, she built a rule book to keep you "safe." That rule book became an unwritten code deeply embedded in your subconscious, one that has controlled your actions—and your life—ever since that first cringeworthy moment you experienced as a child. But this didn't keep you safe; it kept you stuck.

Some of her rules might have become so ingrained in you that now they just feel like an accepted mode of being, or just good, plain common sense. She noticed when you made an outrageous clothing choice for the sixth-grade dance, how that played out, and the pain you felt as a result. So she created a new rule—don't wear anything too weird, different, or loud. Don't stand out; people will stare for all the wrong reasons.

She was there when you raised your hand in class but didn't have the right answer. She heard others giggling, made note of the whispers, and felt the air grow tight and close around you. Another rule was born—always get it right. Don't raise your hand, step forward, or speak up unless you are absolutely certain that your answer is right and that you are going to perform perfectly the moment attention is turned to you.

She stood next to you on the playground when you lost your temper after someone you thought was a friend told you off, and you let them know how you felt about that. She watched as the teacher punished you both equally, and you lost your recess privileges for the rest of the week, even though you were just standing up for yourself. The lesson that was meant for you was also received by your ego, loud and clear. Time for a new rule—be nice, always. Don't cause confrontation. Keep your head down and your mouth shut, even when life is unfair.

As you grew up, her list of rules got longer and longer, like an endless scroll of paper that expands in both directions as far as the eye can see. She couldn't carry a clipboard anymore; there were too many rules. Now she has an internal database that stores an endless amount of information about all the things you have done wrong in your life. And while her intentions were good, her methods were misguided and have

MEET YOUR EGO: YOUR OVERPROTECTIVE BIG SISTER

created a version of you that is very far from your true self. You feel and play small, are hesitant, and constantly question whether you are either too much or not enough. If you're like most women, you've been conditioned to believe that "too much" is when you're voicing your own needs and "not enough" is when you're taking care of the needs of others.

THE ROLE OF THE EGO

If your amygdala is the bodyguard, the ego is the loudest inner narrator in your life. Your ego tells you not to rock the boat or speak up in order to save you from embarrassment. It clings to the old identities that were adopted in childhood, like the good girl, selfless friend, and quiet martyr. Changing those old methods of blending in so that you can stand in yourself threatens the ego's sense of control, causing it to warn you—often as an actual voice inside your head—of the possible negative outcomes.

Have you ever tried to stick up for yourself or set a new boundary only to have an immediate counterargument sprout inside your mind? It might ask—*who do you think you are*? It might tell you that others will judge you for your decision, that you are selfish, or even play out scenarios where you lose a person in your life, or possibly your job, if you draw that line in the sand. This is the normal reaction of the ego; her method of keeping you safe isn't to trigger your in-the-moment fight-or-flight mechanisms, like the amygdala. The ego's role is to exercise control over your actions and decisions that you have time to consider and ponder. But like the amygdala, the ego is protecting you.

Your amygdala and your ego may sound identical, but although they have similar goals, their approach is very different. Let's be sure you know how to identify when each one is at work. Getting to know how these two players in your life operate will help you identify which one is chiming in so that you can be aware of what's going on and make a conscious choice to carve a new path.

HOW THE EGO AND AMYGDALA DIFFER:

The Ego	The Amygdala
Focus: Social Safety (how you look)	Focus: Physical/emotional safety (how you feel/are you "safe"?)
Goal: Be liked, accepted, perfect	Goal: Stay alive, avoid threats
Tone: Critical, judgmental	Tone: Loud, panicked, reactive
Voice of: Perfectionism, comparison, people-pleasing	Voice of: Fight, flight, or freeze response
Personality: Polished, perfection, friend	Personality: Paranoid security guard
Trigger: Uncertainty about social image	Trigger: Perceived threat (physical, emotional, unknown)
Says: Don't look stupid	Says: Run! Danger ahead!
How it feels: Self-doubt, embarrassment, impostor syndrome, comparison	How it feels: Panic, anxiety, racing heart

The amygdala freaks out when you see a mouse or snake, alerting you of physical danger or threats in your environment. The ego freaks out when you go out on a limb via text and don't get a reply. The amygdala reacts to physical threats like lions; the ego reacts to emotional threats like accidently saying the wrong thing in a work meeting or social situation.

MEET YOUR EGO: YOUR OVERPROTECTIVE BIG SISTER

The amygdala tells you to run or fight; the ego tells you to hide or blend in.

The amygdala's job is to keep your body alive, while the ego's job is to keep your identity and social status alive. The ego is more concerned with your reputation than your survival. She measures her success by how you're seen, judged, and whether or not you feel accepted by others. And since she's been with you since you were a little girl, she has a lot to say and some heavily weighted opinions.

The good news is, you are not just your amygdala or ego. They are *parts* of you that you have been living with and possibly beating yourself up over. You have been living your life trying to beat down these powerful inner voices, narrators, and forces in your life. That is the old way, a method of denying parts of yourself that instead you should be working alongside. You can ignite your power by teaming up with your whole self, befriending and creating strength from within. You are no longer going to live life as a fragment of yourself, wondering why you feel the way you do. You're going to learn how to partner with your ego, rewire your brain, and feel safe in the unknown.

It might not always be easy, but it will be worth it.

TOOLS OF THE EGO

Your ego constructed that seemingly endless book of rules, but she has to exercise a set of tools in order to make you adhere to them. Her methods for keeping you safe will probably sound familiar: overanalyzing, perfection, and comparison.

Overanalyzing: If she can't think through and know all possible outcomes, she will just stay small, quiet, or still in order to avoid embarrassment. When the amygdala—your fear center—kicks in, it shuts down your frontal cortex, the logical part of your brain. Essentially, the amygdala makes decisions for you in moments of fear and stress. It decides in a microsecond whether you are going to run or fight. The ego does the opposite; she moves into your frontal cortex and dominates the space, focusing all your thoughts on every possible outcome of any situation, turning each one over and over until it's the only thing you can think about.

Most of the time, she's drawing only on that extensive rule book of all the times in your past when things went wrong if you moved outside your accepted roles of a kind, quiet, self-sacrificing woman that have kept you safe. Often, she comes to the conclusion that taking risks by trying something new or reacting in a different way just isn't worth it—there are too many unknowns. Or she'll wear you down with so many possibilities and outcomes that you are overwhelmed and ultimately choose to do nothing.

If you've ever spent time replaying a conversation over and over in your head, wondering what you could have said differently, and cringing at what you did say, you've experienced your ego throwing her overanalyzing skills around inside your brain. If you've ever hesitated before sending an e-mail, text, posting online, or speaking your truth in public, that's her at work, double-checking you in the moment to make sure you *really* want to do that, and letting you know exactly how it could all go wrong if you do.

Perfection: Your ego knows that the only way to escape all criticism—because let's face it, criticism hurts—is if you, and everything you do, are absolutely perfect. Of course you're not going to post that picture of the piece of clay you molded in your very first pottery class; it's embarrassing. You're not even sure if it's a pitcher or a statue. In fact, you aren't even going to show it to your family—it's that bad. You tried something new and learned that it wasn't worth it. The misshapen clay ends up in the trash, and you probably won't go back for a second class—why would you? You're clearly not good at this. What's even worse is that you wasted time creating a monster when you could have been spending time with your family and meeting their needs. You made a selfish decision, and it didn't pay off. Lesson learned.

Even when you do achieve a measure of success, you self-sabotage, because deep down you know that it's not actually perfect, and whatever you've attempted doesn't deserve praise because it fell short of the goal. Have you ever had your significant other compliment what you made for dinner, only to find yourself responding, "Thank you, but it needs more salt"? What about that outfit that your best friend complimented, but you just *had* to point out that it's a little snug around the waist?

The truth is that perfection is unattainable; it's not real. But the ego doesn't know that. She just knows about all the times in the past when you fell short, and it was a painful experience. So she'll keep pushing you to strive for the impossible because her goal is to save you from embarrassment, and being perfect is the only way to achieve that.

Comparison: If you've ever been on social media, you know this feeling. Everyone has fuller hair, a bigger butt, clearer skin, whiter teeth, and sparklier eyes. Your ego immediately assesses all these (often filtered) images in order to measure you against others to determine where you figure in. She is constantly assessing the group and reminding you that even though you are most definitely *not* at the top of the pile—because that's perfection and you are certainly not that—you can still participate by showing up and fitting in so that others will accept you. Often, this means smothering your authentic self and trying to maintain a space within a group that you don't actually belong in.

Online platforms are only the newest and fastest way to make you feel like you're not living up to standards. Even if you have taken yourself offline in order to preserve your sanity, there are still plenty of reminders in our culture that you don't have what other women do. Billboards, magazine covers, TV shows, and movies, even actual real people moving through the world in front of you, are all material for your ego to devour and use as examples of how you're falling short.

And these are just examples of your ego using comparison of your physical features to those of others. She's also aware of bigger houses, newer cars, larger diamonds, and higher-performing kids. You can even fail outside of the material world. Your ego takes notice when someone else is funnier, faster, stronger, smarter, and just plain *better* than you. She takes note of all these things and files them away . . . and she'll be sure to trot them out as a reminder the next time you consider trying something new or changing things up.

After hearing all of this, you may think that she is here to make you miserable, but remember your ego was born out of love and protection—she is simply here to keep you safe. She wants you to belong, but her misguided methods keep you adapting to the group, masking your true self. She doesn't know that helping you to avoid pain and embarrassment has also kept you playing small and staying stuck. It's also kept you tightly wound and anxious, hiding the most special and unique aspects of yourself and having way less fun.

But that's all going to change. Hang tight.

THE VOICE THAT WHISPERS

I need to introduce you to one more player in this game of your internal life. While your ego likely shows up as the loudest voice, she's not the only one narrating. There is another voice, one that whispers. She's quiet and harder to hear, but she speaks from the wisdom of every woman who has come before you for hundreds and thousands of years. She is your true self.

While ego is all about protection, true self is all about lightness and freedom. She is feminine, she is soft, she is free, and she is flowing. While ego is cautious, true self is grounded in the confidence from a lineage of powerful women. Ego cares what people think. True self pays no mind—she knows her worth is rooted in who she is, not what other people think of her. You may not realize it, but you already know her, too. She is the one who gently nudges you to speak what's in your heart.

Many of us have let ego sit in the driver's seat for so long that we have forgotten that our true self can get us to the same destination—most likely providing a much more enjoyable ride in the process. For much of our lives we have spent a ridiculous amount of time playing an exhausting game of internal tug-of-war, never really knowing which version of ourselves to lead with. While one pulls us toward safety and familiarity, the other nudges us toward personal growth and new experiences. Your ego warns you not to speak up, while your true self assures you that your voice is important. Your ego tells you that applying for a new job will only result in rejection and embarrassment, while your true self says that you deserve this and are capable of much more than you think.

You spend much of your time toggling between these two inner personalities, often without realizing it. Every decision you make throughout your day begins with a subconscious choice about which version of you will lead the way. Every time you let one speak over the other, you are showing up as a half version of yourself. Only half of you is attempting to go full speed ahead in your busy life; only half of you is trying to accomplish the endless to-do list—no wonder you're exhausted!

INTRODUCING THE WHOLE SELF

This internal battle and game of tug-of-war isn't a flaw, it's just a human behavior. Your goal should not be to suppress or somehow get past your ego. Although many thought leaders have touted this as the way, you are no longer going to aim to smother part of yourself. Instead, ignite power from within by combining these two forces and forming an alliance. This will be the greatest partnership you have ever experienced, allowing you to show up as your whole self.

There may have been glimmers of showing up as your whole self at some point in your life. Maybe it was when you took a big risk at work, or went after that guy you had a crush on, or anything in between. Living from your whole self feels like coming home, producing a profound sense of ease and inner connection, authenticity, and peace. It's the rare times in your life when you feel your head, heart, and gut are all on the same page. There is no tug-of-war or push-and-pull deciding which version of you wins. Moving from this place feels like a quiet certainty, like the world is moving with you, not against.

Chances are, you've already experienced this but didn't have a name for it. There are likely moments in your life when you acted on a gut feeling that guided you in making a

MEET YOUR EGO: YOUR OVERPROTECTIVE BIG SISTER

decision that didn't make logical sense at the time. You trusted it and later realized it was exactly the right choice. Similarly, if you've experienced a flow state—being so immersed in whatever is in front of you that time ceases to exist—you are likely acting as your whole self. When you're fully in the moment and don't have a second thought about how you look, what others think, or what you need to do next, you are moving as your whole self.

If you've ever spoken up for yourself without overthinking it, you've been there. It might be rare, but there has surely been an instance or two where you unapologetically asked for what you needed—no backpedaling, no guilt. Those moments when you knew exactly what you needed and advocated for yourself were times when your whole self was present. Remember how great that felt? What about times when you have allowed yourself to be fully seen and felt safe showing up as your messy, emotional, unhinged, and vulnerable whole self? These are priceless experiences and great indicators that the people you were with in those moments are the ones you trust to love you, no matter what.

Others can help you experience your true self through feelings of intense gratitude as well. Those moments of pure appreciation, when you're acknowledging that life isn't perfect—but dammit, it's still pretty great—are beautiful. Maybe it's when your kids are sleeping and you stare at their little faces, feeling so thankful for them. It may have also shown up when you were experiencing something very simple but profound, and you paused and noticed a warm, expansive feeling in your chest.

Moments of peace amid chaos are also powerful evidence that you are in touch with your whole self. Your amygdala can't win every time! You've certainly experienced moments of high stress where you kept a strong foundational center and remained grounded. You found a quiet inner power that you aligned with, while keeping your breath steady and your heart calm. Your whole self may even be in control and acting in ways that you are not aware of. These are called synchronicities—times when everything seems to magically line up. You need something and it appears. You were missing someone and they called you. It may seem as if the universe is directly stepping into your path, but the truth is that it's a powerful force inside of you that this emanates from.

You can know for sure that you are living from your whole self when your body feels light, calm, and connected. Life feels effortless and easy, and you're getting it all done without feeling rushed, stressed, or spread too thin. You feel a quiet sense of self-confidence that enables you to make choices that are aligned with your values, and you do so without second-guessing because you trust yourself.

This isn't some rare fluke or unattainable phenomenon. That ease, that flow—that's your natural state. And it happens more often when you're in alignment with your whole self. Here's the most beautiful part: It's not about doing more. It's about letting go and getting realigned. Alignment with your whole self isn't something you chase or force. It's something you allow. And the more you lean into it, the more life will begin to flow—not through effort but through ease.

Something magical happens when you approach your life from your whole self—you stop waiting. You stop waiting for the right moment to show up before taking action. You stop waiting for peace and groundedness to find you. You stop wishing the week away so that you can finally catch your breath. When you connect with your whole self, you realize that everything you have ever needed has always been inside of you, just waiting for you to come home. You stop outsourcing your calm—no more searching outside of you for validation, approval, permission, or power. Sounds beautiful, doesn't it?!

This is the beginning of our battle cry. It's our call to reject the old rules of self-care and embrace the new model, the one that we design together as today's fully realized women. One that doesn't just promise calm by putting a carrot out in front of us that we chase, just hoping we can get to the finish line so we can finally enjoy a moment to ourselves. This version is deliverable on demand. It doesn't require time, money, or waiting for the right moment to occur. It's time to break free from the outdated model of self-care and connect with our power from within.

Ladies, our revolution starts now.

REFLECTIVE EXERCISES AND PRACTICES

THE SAFE VS. STUCK CHART:

Category	Safe (true protection)	Stuck (fear masking as safety)
Career/Passions		
Relationships		
Parenting		
Health and Wellness		
Personal Growth		
Social Life		
Dreams and Goals		

HOW TO USE THIS CHART:

1. Reflect on your life, and identify and list what actions you are taking to genuinely keep yourself *safe*, vs. what limitations you believe are keeping you safe but when you think on it more deeply, are actually keeping you stuck.

2. Identify patterns and limiting beliefs: Are there areas where you are repeatedly choosing familiar pain over unknown possibility?

3. Choose one area where you are STUCK and focus on it this week. Commit to one action step that will help propel you forward.

Examples:

- Career/Passions: Submit an application for that dream job that feels out of reach. Look for a class for something you have always been interested in and sign up.

- Relationships: Plan on one authentic and perhaps even vulnerable, open, and truly connected conversation you will have this week. This could be with a partner, a loved one, your child, or maybe that woman you have been wanting to become friends with.

- Parenting: Is there a parenting method you have been hearing about that you are curious to try? Try it without judgment and without attaching yourself to the result. The win is you simply being willing to take a step forward and not being focused on potential imperfections.

- Health and Wellness: Want to start going to the gym in the morning? Create your plan for success. Put your gym clothes out the night before, find a class you'd love to try, team up with an accountability buddy—whatever helps you take that step forward.

- Personal Growth: Start journaling for five minutes a day, join a book club or an online community committed to growth, try breathwork or meditation, limit time on social media by tracking it.
- Social life: This may look like saying yes to something that feels scary. This may also look like saying no to social events and circles that no longer serve you.
- Dreams and Goals: Take the first step on a project in your home or get clear on what you want to create space for in your life. Be open to options that are less about adding more to-dos to your list and perhaps more about how you want to *be*—adding more calm, connection, family time, and balance.

CHAPTER 3

The Myths of Womanhood

Womanhood is full of myths (outdated beliefs, false truths, conditioned scripts, silent agreements, limiting narratives). Some of them are much-ingrained lessons of the patriarchy that were put in place long ago to ensure women remained second-class citizens. Thankfully, in the modern age, many of us have learned how to identify those built-in parameters and throw off that mantle. But there are other myths of womanhood that have held on longer, mostly because they are well-meaning mantras that have always been looked upon as accepted truths, even though they are causing damage.

Society hands us these perfectly packaged truths with a wink and a nudge, as if we are being imparted age-old wisdom that weaves through the generations of women who came before us. As if these are the universal keys to doing things the right way and being happy while we do them. But in actuality, the only thing these so-called truths do is encourage burnout, introduce guilt, induce shame, and bring about a deep feeling of failure, making many of us wonder what in the world is wrong with us as individuals, since other women as a group seem to be sailing along fine. Hint: They're not.

Let's unpack some of these outdated myths and laugh (or cry) a bit in order to explore how reconnecting with your whole self is the actual key to your happiness, not a door that opens onto the same place you've always been—that stuck place you're trying to get out of.

MYTH 1: PUT YOUR OXYGEN MASK ON FIRST!

This one's a classic and I am fully on board with the concept—but it needs some tweaking. Yes, it's true, and even the flight attendants on a plane reinforce it with their in-flight safety briefing. And while that is likely the place where you've heard this phrase used the most, let's establish what it means outside of emergency situations.

If we don't take care of ourselves (put our oxygen mask on first), we won't be able to assist others. It's a long-standing maxim that you can find in just about every self-help book concerning parenting, marriage, and probably even friendship. It's often shared at least once a week in an Instagram post by someone who looks perfect, reinforcing the message and likely doubling down on a particular product that can help you do exactly that. But what *is* your real-life oxygen mask? What do you imagine you're supposed to do anytime someone says this to you? Buy that foot massager or miracle cream for your hands? Carve out a day at the spa? Attend a yoga retreat in Bali? Have a day to yourself? Lock yourself in a soundproof room and engage in some primal screaming for half an hour?

Let's be real—most of the tools we've been taught belong in our self-care toolbox are either too expensive to be feasible for the everyday woman or take up more time than we have to give. The methods of self-care that are espoused today are commercial and designed to put money in someone else's pocket, while taking it out of yours. Time constraints are also real, and giving yourself that day at the spa is often at the bottom of a long to-do list. Even if you are able to squeeze it in, that means something else got bumped, and now you're going to stress out about that. This approach often does nothing other than make us feel like we're failing at yet another thing; we literally can't even take care of ourselves properly.

Social media does not help. You might scroll and see beautifully put-together women talking about the importance of a morning to themselves in order to get their best start to the day. They encourage you to get some sun, meditate, journal, work out, set your goals, and *then* start your day. That sounds wonderful, doesn't it? But what about the mom who wakes up to kids instantly needing her? What about the woman who has to leave for work before the sun is even up? What about the woman working two jobs to make the rent, who needs to sleep right up until it's time to walk out the door?

We need a New Age oxygen mask. We don't need phrases and motivational quotes plastered all over social media. We need tools that work amid our meltdowns, something we can cling to when our nervous system is sounding the alarm. We've been taught that the oxygen masks to reach for are the girls' night, the pedicure, the massage, the hour away. And those things aren't bad. I happen to love them all. But they are the *macro* things—the big options. We need something easier, something in real time that brings us back to ourselves in the moment. We need the ability to microdose self-care through moments of connection.

Before I discovered the whole-self connection code, I fell prey to these messages as well. I wanted to do everything

I was supposed to be doing—including carving out that me-time in the morning. I was managing my career while raising and homeschooling three kids, which meant that I had to be ready to be a full-on mom and career woman by 7 A.M. I'm sure many of you reading this can relate. So how did I create that oh-so-special me-time so that I could have it all? By getting up at 4 A.M., of course!

I woke up exhausted. My body begged for more sleep, sometimes literally. I swear I could hear a little whisper warning me that this wasn't the answer; this wasn't good for me. I shut her up real fast with strong coffee, then drove to a 5 A.M. CrossFit class, complete with bright lights, loud music, and lots of metal for me to throw around. I was dedicated to getting a PR (personal record) or as many reps as possible on my deadlifts, or another Olympic weight-lifting move—even though my body still hurt from what I'd put it through the day before. After that super-constructive, having-it-all power hour, I'd go home and start breakfast for everyone. I was putting my oxygen mask on first. I was doing it right.

Or was I kidding myself? Was I actually wearing myself down to nothing with this routine that was supposedly good for me? Is it any wonder that my body finally collapsed, unable to keep up with the demands I was putting on it . . . the ones that popular culture told me were necessary, even helpful?

You might be in the same place. You might feel stretched to the max, pushed to your limits, and on the verge of a breakdown. You might even do what I did—ignore the small voice inside, trying to tell you that something has to change, that you need to stop. For me, the breaking point came with a major illness. It could be the same for you, or it could be any number of other things, such as a mental health crisis or an autoimmune condition.

We don't need to be tasked with doing more in order to have our needs met. What most women need is something that is quick, easy, and effective. This is where the whole-self concept fits in. Rather than being another item on your to-do list, this helps you realign with who you already are in just a few minutes a day. Think of it as the oxygen you already have inside your lungs, not as an outside source that you have to seek out, pay for, and make time for.

MYTH 2: ASK FOR HELP!

Ha-ha, oh sure, let me just call up my village and have them swoop in with some casseroles and free childcare. The reality is that everyone is struggling. Everyone's plate is full. All of us feel like we are just trying to survive the chaos. Your never-ending list of to-dos is just as long as that of your neighbor, sister, best friend, or parent. According to Motherly's 2021 State of Motherhood survey, 93 percent of mothers feel like they are burned out.[4] And a write-up by Accesswire from July 21, 2023, mentions a survey that found that 68 percent of mothers feel crippling anxiety about the pressure to be perfect (there's that word again) and that 71 percent face financial strains.[5] *Fast Company* cites similar concerns, mentioning in the article that "working mothers across America are fed up; battling scheduling, childcare, pay gaps, and guilt . . . enough is enough."[6] Asking another woman for help often just seems as if you are handing your overloaded pile to someone who is buried under their own. Even asking feels like an admission of failure on your part.

Let's say you do reach the end of your rope and ask someone else for help. There are only two possibilities of how that plays out. The first is that they say yes, of course, I am happy to help you out. There are a lot of wonderful people on the planet who truly are givers and welcome the opportunity to relieve the stress of others. But . . . that doesn't mean you'll feel good about taking them up on it. Chances are this will only induce guilt on your part, and you'll constantly feel as if you are in debt to them—even if they don't see it that way.

There's also the possibility that they will say no, because they are also just as worn out, overworked, and exhausted as you are. They might even produce their own list of to-dos to illustrate exactly how busy they are to validate their decision to turn you down. When this happens, you not only feel guilt, but also an additional helping of shame. She just showed you exactly how much she's got going on in her life, yet *she's* managing it. She didn't ask *you* for help, did she? She's making it happen. Why can't you?

I can remember times that I asked for extra help with the kids so that I could meet a work deadline, then felt *double* the amount of guilt. Not only did I prioritize work over family, but I also asked someone else to prioritize my family over their own! Who does that? Not a good mom or friend, that's for sure. The end result is that I would sit at work feeling guilt and shame, not being productive. In other words, completely undermining myself. And what happened next? The ego made a note of how asking for help plays out—and she reminded me of that terrible feeling the next time I felt overwhelmed, causing me to remain small, stuck, and isolated.

Luckily, there is a new way. Asking for help can look different from what we imagine. Shame, guilt, and that pervasive feeling of failure are avoidable. We can remind our ever-present ego when she chimes in that it's safe to ask for help. Doing so can actually benefit another person by giving them a deepened sense of purpose. We all love to feel helpful and to experience a sense of contribution. A crucial element of the whole-self connection code is to learn how to identify what your ego is doing and to develop the ability to sort through it logically.

MYTH 3: IT TAKES A VILLAGE!

Pretty sure we're all fully aware of this, but that knowledge isn't exactly helpful. We know we are juggling more than is realistic for one woman to handle. Career, home, marriage, meal planning, and our social calendars are enough to make a person's head spin. Some of us can add to this the never-ending to-dos of raising children: homework, fundraisers, spirit week, parent-teacher meetings . . . and also, of course, keeping the offspring clothed, fed, sheltered, clean, and hopefully functioning mentally and emotionally. Yes, we know this is all too much for one person—that's very clear. But where is this village everyone speaks of? Where do we find one?

We may be surrounded by people—partners, co-workers, friends, other parents, and maybe even our book club or regular ladies' night meetup. We can hop online and interact with people we know in real life and those we don't. But despite the high level of connectivity available to us, we are more isolated than ever. A 2024 survey by the American Psychiatric Association found that at least 30 percent of adult Americans said they experienced loneliness several times a week.[7] The village that's supposed to help us raise our children simply doesn't exist anymore, because our way of living has changed in the modern age.

We rarely experience the depth of a true connection that the women who came before us took for granted. As women we are communal beings. We have a deeply rooted biological and physiological need for connection, collaboration, and support of one another. In our hunting and gathering days, our survival depended on the strength of our community. Women worked together to care for their children, gather food, and provide for the group. We shared duties that were essential for creating a stable and thriving environment. Communal living meant that everyone shared resources, time, and whatever small comforts could be had in the day to day.

The modern world simply no longer functions this way; our village is gone. Today, we live in isolated nuclear families, and the workload that used to be spread among many now rests heavily on the shoulders of an individual. Our traditional sense of community is fractured, and the near-constant presence of tech means that our connection with other humans is often taking a backseat to our need for screens. Think about the last time you were able to grab a girls' night or get-together with friends. How often was someone—maybe even you—dropping out of the conversation to look at their phone?

The truth is we cannot give another what we won't give ourselves. How can we create or participate in a village if we can't even sit with ourselves? I have to make a conscious effort in the few moments of downtime between daily tasks to not grab my phone—how about you? Before I learned how to connect with my whole self, I saw any moment of stillness as an opportunity to fill it with something else. Have a car ride alone? Throw on a podcast or call and catch up with a friend.

What about just creating space to let my mind wander? Or even just have a conversation with the person in my life who is neglected the most—myself? This lack of ability to connect with ourselves is a big factor in our lack of connection with others. In isolating ourselves from our own voices, we have lost the ability to build community. The village of our ancestors, which was critical to not only survival, but happiness, is a thing of the past.

That loss of communal living means that we are more stressed as individuals—and as parents—than ever before. In fact, we've moved so far from that mode of living that those who still practice it sometimes face legal ramifications. Free-range parenting gives children more freedom and allows them room to grow and have larger experiences outside of their homes and schools without parental oversight. Inherent in that concept is the idea that other adults will still be present and can intervene in the role of a parent if necessary. However, there are many states where parents of free-range children can be charged with child neglect, when in reality they're just living out the age-old adage—but the village doesn't exist anymore.

The whole-self approach helps us create deeper connections with others by first creating a connection with ourselves. It will help you tune in to your needs, desires, and values, so that you can identify what's necessary for you (that oxygen mask) in order for you to be a functioning member of a group. With the whole-self approach, you'll learn how to set boundaries that will attract people who share those needs, desires, and values, and you can begin to build that village we all so desperately want and have lost.

MYTH 4: ENJOY EVERY MOMENT, IT GOES SO FAST!

Really? EVERY moment? How about the one where I'm late to work, forgot my lunch, hit a traffic jam, and definitely didn't have the chance to floss. Also, I have my period, because of course I do. Is this a moment I should enjoy?

Have you ever been vulnerable enough to share with someone that you are struggling—whether you're an exhausted mother or a single woman juggling career, friendships, and dating—only to have someone tell you to enjoy what you have? What I'm having is a nervous breakdown, thanks. No, I'm not enjoying it. And now you just made me feel bad about the fact that I feel bad. Cue the downward cycle of internal shame—and, oh, by the way, your big sister ego just made a note that a little bit of venting results in being made to feel worse, not better. Noted—suffer in silence.

Along with the guilt sandwich that was just handed to you, you're being met with the assumption that every struggle and challenge should feel meaningful and fulfilling. If it doesn't, the problem isn't that life is overwhelming and the modern age is isolating—the actual problem is you, not enjoying every single moment of torment and loneliness. For so many women who are pulled in too many directions, some moments simply aren't enjoyable. They're overwhelming, frustrating, and exhausting.

I've had my moments of vulnerability where I shared my stress, frustration, and overwhelm, only to have my hand slapped by being told that I should be thankful for every moment because kids grow up fast, and I'll miss it all someday. Implied in these statements is the idea that I don't see my children as blessings, that I don't love them enough, and—worst of all—that I am being a selfish mother. It's as if I were out in the ocean drowning, waving for help, only to have the person on the beach yell, "But it's such a beautiful day! Aren't you grateful to be able to spend it in the ocean?"

Instead of being told to enjoy every complicated, fraught moment along with the beautiful ones, what you actually need is to be validated in your struggle. To be met with love, support, and connection. The whole-self approach shifts your focus away from trying to *enjoy* every moment to meeting these moments with authenticity, compassion for—and connection to—ourselves.

MYTH 5: THE PERFECT WOMAN EXISTS!

This is less of what someone says to you and more of a theme that certainly pops up everywhere. The one that feeds your ego's tool of comparison and gives you even more reason to feel like you aren't measuring up. Maybe it's someone you saw on social media whose home is clean, white, minimal, and bright. She makes everything look so damn easy and effortless. Her outfits are always on point, her hair and makeup stellar, her relationships appear perfect, and she is the one you compare yourself to whenever you're on the struggle bus. She's managing, you're not.

Spoiler alert: She's not real. Spoiler follow-up: You are.

The myth of the perfect woman has been passed down through magazine covers, Instagram filters, Pinterest, and Facebook posts. She's the one whose kids are reading every night, doing all their chores, eating their well-balanced meals, and actually flossing. The truth is that perfection is unattainable, but that doesn't stop us from exhausting ourselves while we chase it.

Instead of striving for perfection, what if we started aiming for connection?

What if we worried less about the dishes in the sink and the growing pile of laundry and instead decided to be fully present in the moment, either by ourselves or with other people? What if we prioritized relaxing when we need it, rather than when we finally manage that one last thing on the to-do list? By the way, we all know there is never one last thing. That's just today's list. Tomorrow will be refilled with dishes, laundry, trash, and food preparation. What if we decided to stop seeing how much work we can get done and instead start working on our ability to stop, pivot, and connect in any moment—even the most chaotic ones.

Before I learned how to connect with my whole self, I was a woman tearing through her to-do list, promising myself that once all the boxes were ticked, I would spend time with my family or put my feet up. I was an expert at distracting myself right out of any connection with what I actually desired, wanted, or even flat-out needed in order to survive. I was constantly in motion, wanting everything to be a certain way before I could just *be*.

Shifting into the whole-self approach will help you show up as your authentic, true, and imperfect self, the version of you that your husband married, your children love, and who doesn't have 10.2k followers on Instagram. The one who isn't a raging ball of stress because she has spent every minute running around finishing tasks. The one who is okay with some crumbs on the counter and a few dishes in the sink. The one who is maybe a little bit wild, free, and able to let it all go. That's the version of you that the people who love you need most.

MYTH 6: YOU CAN HAVE IT ALL!

Let's take a closer look at this one, shall we? Having it all so often equates to a list of success metrics that are typically based on external validation as a reminder of our worth. A thriving career, an immaculate home, Pinterest-worthy family meals, date nights, the perfect body, a daily meditation, journaling, and gratitude practice. Does this sound fulfilling, or does it sound like a one-way ticket to burnout?

What is needed is a paradigm shift. What if we reframed *having it all* to *being it all*?

Our society puts a lot of value on outcomes like how much money our job puts in the bank, as opposed to whether or not we actually like going to work. We need to focus less on accomplishing things and more on considering how we feel during the process. How we show up in our lives and behave and interact with our loved ones is a greater indicator of worth than anything else. It's not easily measured, but that doesn't mean it's a less valid way to live. You can learn how to make your way through your daily goals by first asking yourself not *what do I need to do today?* but rather, *how do I want to feel while I'm doing it?* The pressure of *having* it all will be released, and you'll realize that instead *being* it all is the real reward.

As a busy woman with a career and three children, I've had my fair share of nights when I felt exhausted, but as soon as I lay down, my brain wanted to let me know everything I *didn't* accomplish that day, and also remind me that I hadn't spent enough time with my kids either. After learning how to approach the day as my whole self, I put my head on the pillow, not asking if I got everything *done*, but rather how I showed up as I was doing it. It's a sense of satisfaction like no other. Not only can I get things done, but—more importantly—I don't snap at my kids because they're keeping me from the next to-do. I've learned how to be at peace and still accomplish things.

It's a total game changer.

THE EXPECTATION OF FAILURE

The common denominator in all of these well-meaning mantras is that they set you up for failure. They create expectations that are impossible to adhere to . . . but it seems like other people are managing it, so you decide that you must be the problem.

You're not. These myths are.

By pivoting away from these myths and reconnecting to your whole self, you shift from a state of doing to being. Life will no longer be about finding the perfect elusive village; it will be about creating micro-moments and opportunities of alignment and connection that fit into the life you already have. Whether you are a mom, an aunt, a caretaker, career woman, housewife, or simply someone navigating the modern world as a busy woman, these tools are for you.

So laugh or cry; just make sure you release it—along with these ridiculous sayings. Know you are not alone, we're all fed up and ready for a new way, a new system that actually works with us and for us. One that reminds us that we don't have to do it all or even enjoy it all; we simply need to show up as we are, and that's more than enough.

REFLECTIVE EXERCISES AND PRACTICES

Sit down with your journal and identify times in your life when you have come up against each of these myths. Write out how it made you feel or how you reacted—even if it's messy. Then, reread what you wrote, considering your words through the lens of self-acceptance. The next time you encounter these myths, you'll have the tools to navigate them differently.

CHAPTER 4

Be. Do. Have.

Now that you've uncovered the myths of womanhood—the outdated, well-meaning, yet ultimately harmful advice passed down like ancient wisdom—you might feel the weight of just how much has been holding you back. These so-called truths weren't designed to empower us; they were survival strategies for a different time, and most of them never worked as well as we were led to believe. But imagine this: Somewhere, beyond the noise of those myths, there are whispers—quiet, intuitive guidance from the women who came before us. Women who lived in alignment, who knew how to create lives of meaning, abundance, and joy, and who are ready to show you the way. From a place inside you where your whole self lives, you maintain a deep reservoir of instinctual knowledge. If you take the time to listen, you can hear her inviting you to take a drink.

The Be-Do-Have formula is her gift to you—a blueprint for breaking free and stepping into your power. This isn't just about moving forward; it's about moving forward with intention, clarity, and the kind of wisdom that feels like homecoming. Let's leave behind the myths and step into the truth together.

✳ ✳ BE. DO. HAVE. ✳ ✳

Why does success feel just out of reach, no matter how hard you work? How is it possible that you can tick off the to-do list—and maybe even get it all done—but still not feel like you've accomplished anything, or come any closer to the goal? It's because most of us are playing by the wrong rules—chasing what we want to *have* (money, love, success) before becoming the person capable of creating it.

This is where the Be-Do-Have formula steps in. The not-so-secret secret behind manifestation, the law of attraction, and how life really works. This isn't woo-woo; it's the practical, proven way to create anything you want—aligned, authentic, and on your terms. By the end of this chapter, you'll understand this formula and discover the clarity, ease, and pure bliss of finally stepping into alignment with your desires.

LIES MY LIFE TOLD ME

From the time we are young children, we are programmed to believe that *having* the right things—good grades, a big trophy, the best clothes—will unlock happiness, belonging, and success. As adults, society does a great job of reinforcing this by bombarding us with these messages through advertising, media, and famous spokespeople. You're sad? Eat ice cream! You want to look like a supermodel? Follow her fitness routine! Still not happy with your body? These clothes can fix that! Western culture ingrains in us that external sources can fix whatever is wrong with us on the inside . . . you just have to get enough money to buy happiness.

Beyond buying products, our society also tells us other ways that external sources are going to fill the void. A college degree will gain you that dream job. Being married will give you a feeling of safety. Having children will make you whole. Losing weight will give you more confidence. And once you've managed to do all the things required in order to achieve that (probably by buying products or subscribing to an influencer's social media), you'll be able to spend quality time with your friends and family.

This messaging is strong, pervasive, and insidious. It hides in every corner of our lives, pushing us to *have* more in order to *be* happy. It's no wonder we have been approaching everything from the wrong angle, falling short, then looking for a product that can help us be better at . . . buying the products that will make us happy. You are not failing; the system is designed to keep you spinning on your hamster wheel, spending money so that the economy is healthy—but *you* are not.

You were conditioned to believe that the next milestone, purchase, or accomplishment would fix everything. This model of Have-Do-Be—you need to *have* certain products in order to *do* the things that will make you *be* happy—feels logical in a culture that rewards external achievements and possession of material things. But here's the problem, and it's a big one—this approach keeps you trapped and stuck in a perpetual cycle of waiting. Waiting to feel good, waiting to be enough, waiting for others to fulfill you, waiting for the perfect situation to arise so you can finally be happy. This puts all the power and influence outside of you. You are destined to be let down, disappointed, and set up for a feeling of having no control in your life.

The truth is transformation flows from inside of you. You have the ability to create the life of your dreams. I know that might sound crazy, especially after spending so much of your life falling short and feeling like a failure. But remember—you have been living life by the wrong rules. You have been living life by the same broken formula, yet hoping and praying for a different outcome every time it is repackaged and sold to you from a slightly different angle. Flipping the script and leaning into the Be-Do-Have model is what will allow you to finally experience the life you were meant to have, the one that's already inside of you, waiting to be let out.

This might feel like just another recycled self-help ideology, another system you'll try only to end up feeling like you've failed. But I promise you, as a woman who has walked the same path you're on—this is different. The Be-Do-Have formula isn't about stressing and forcing a new way of life or adding more to your already full plate. I would never do that to you, because I know what my plate looks like! It's about starting where you are—right now—with small, courageous steps that are doable, not overwhelming. With each step, each shift, you'll begin to notice something—clarity, ease, and maybe even a spark of joy. As these moments build, they'll carry you forward. Before you know it, this way of living will feel as natural as breathing, and the life you once dreamed about will start unfolding.

So take a deep breath, and let's start small, together.

FLIPPING YOUR SCRIPT: THE BE-DO-HAVE PRINCIPLE

When you start with *being*, your actions align effortlessly with your goals. Imagine that confident friend, family member, co-worker in your life. She naturally does things like speak up for herself, set boundaries, or try out new things. She creates her own life—the one you admire . . . and you might be a little jealous of. It all starts with who she chooses to *be*, and you can create that, too. Remember, it won't look exactly like hers does; that's not the goal. It shouldn't be, because you are crafting something that is entirely personal, entirely yours.

Making this shift is simple, but it's not necessarily easy. Let's unpack what makes it difficult so that you can understand why other approaches you have tried may have failed in the past. Aspects from previous programming and conditioning present challenges in your future because you have been conditioned in certain ways.

The first—and often most powerful—aspect is cultural programming that began from a young age and likely permeated your upbringing. From the beginning, external validation was necessary in order for you to feel worthy. Did you need your mom or dad's approval before you could feel like you had accomplished something or done it well enough? Were you constantly assessing your siblings so that you could be the *good* one, winning the praise and coming out on top? That comparison model is deeply entrenched and continues to be reinforced by all the cultural messaging we've already discussed through marketing and social media.

As humans, we have a deep desire to avoid discomfort. Taking a new path will often make you feel vulnerable, even awkward. This is where your ego jumps in with the warning that unfamiliar things could be dangerous, and it would be safer (easier) to fall back into your old patterns than lean into a new change.

Instant gratification plays a large part in the failure to new approaches. We live in a society of quick fixes. Need that wrinkle cream right now? No problem, sign up for Amazon Prime. Want to watch the entire season of that brand-new show everyone is talking about? Of course you do, and it's available on this streaming service that you can subscribe to. (Notice how you're spending money? Yep. Thanks, old model). A new path requires you to understand from the beginning that this will take time and effort but will eventually bring about an efficient form of self-care. This is the long game, and you'll need to play it with the awareness that short-term solutions might seem attractive, but they ultimately leave you feeling empty.

HOW TO SHIFT INTO THE BE-DO-HAVE MINDSET:

Step 1: Identify What You Want to Have

Start by thinking about what you want to achieve or possess. It's okay to begin with the old way of thinking—we're going to reverse-engineer it. What you want to have can be material objects, an emotional goal with your family or friends, or a mental place you'd like to create for yourself. Don't limit yourself—dream big!

Step 2: Visualize Someone Who Already Has It

Imagine someone who embodies this goal. It could be someone you know, or you can create a detailed vision of this person in your mind, an avatar of your future self. Close your eyes and imagine:

- Their demeanor: How do they carry themselves?
- Their habits and routines: What does their day-to-day life look like?
- Their choices: How do they spend their time, handle challenges, and interact with others?
- Their environment: Who do they spend time with? What activities fill their day?

Next, think about this person's actions and reactions, describing them in as much detail as possible:

- How do they start and end their day?
- What do they do if they face stress or distractions?
- How do they align their actions with their goals?

Step 3: Compare Their Behaviors to Your Own

Be brutally honest with yourself. Look at your current habits, routines, and behaviors. Identify what (or who) might be interfering with your ability to align with the version of yourself who has what you want.

- What are your current habits, routines, and behaviors that don't align with the person you described above?

Step 4: Choose Your First Small Swaps

Start small. Practice low-hanging fruit changes to begin shifting toward alignment. What are five small swaps you can make this week to start behaving differently? Consider the elements listed below if you need something to get you started:

- Morning and night routines
- Meal decisions
- Screen time limits
- New reading/listening materials
- Boundaries you can set

Step 5: Make a Promise to Yourself

This is where the magic happens. Reflect on why this change matters and what it will feel like to achieve it.

- What's on the other side for you?
- Why is this so important?
- How will it feel to make it happen this time?

Step 6: Set Yourself Up for Success

Accountability is key. Join a community or connect with a partner who has walked this path and can stretch you.

- Who can you link up with to help you stay on track?
- What community can you join to surround yourself with people on the same journey?

Step 7: Take On a New Identity

When I need a bit of courage while trying a new way, I literally pretend I'm someone else. If you want to speak up for yourself but can't find your own voice, it might help to pretend for a moment that you're that sassy friend Sheila who asks for what she needs without apology. You're not taking on Sheila's identity but reflecting on her behaviors and how they mirror your own values and goals.

MEET THE MIDLIFE GYMNAST

I have been utilizing the Be-Do-Have principle for the past two decades of my life. In doing so I can say I have created the life of my dreams, but that doesn't mean I had no regrets. Growing up I was a gymnast, and I loved it. Often when I was in line waiting for my turn on the vault or to tumble, I would look around the gymnasium, powerfully aware of the years of opportunities that lay ahead of me, the entire lifetime I had at my disposal to become better at something I loved, something that made both my body and my heart feel good.

Unfortunately, that wasn't enough to overcome my innate shyness. Once I made the team, a great fear of performing in front of people got the best of me. I also wasn't on the same page as my coach but lacked the courage to advocate for myself and ask for what I needed in order to feel comfortable. Rather than address my performance anxiety or create boundaries with my coach, I quit. I quit something I loved out of fear. A deep sense of failure followed me throughout my adulthood as a result, but I chose to ignore it, as I believed that my opportunity to participate was in the past.

The feeling resurfaced in my 40s. I ended up back in a gymnasium, this time as a mom instead of a participant. Something else was different, too. I'd been practicing the Be-Do-Have principle for years and had learned how to go after what I wanted. So I decided—*oh, why the hell not?* I approached my kids' gymnastics coach and asked if he would train a 42-year-old woman. Surprisingly, he was elated—the gym was starting an adult class the following week! I signed up and once again got to walk into a gymnasium, put chalk dust on my hands, and feel the power of my own body. The disappointed child inside me stretched her limbs and found freedom.

Not only did I start training every week, but my coach also encouraged me to participate in a competition the gym was hosting . . . where all the other athletes were 12 and under. I immediately said no, then realized that I was enacting an old pattern—stepping back because of embarrassment or shame. I reconsidered, said yes, and went on to accomplish something I denied my 11-year-old self. Not only did the other parents support me, many of the women approached me to let me know how inspired they were by my choice. I even ran into a gym dad a week later at a gas station, and he let me know how impressed his young daughters were. I walked away from the conversation with a deep sense of pride, not because of what I had accomplished, but because I had practiced what I preached! I modeled Be-Do-Have for everyone: the tired moms who might want to pick up piano again but don't think they have time, and the little girls who will grow up, feel overwhelmed, and remember the "old lady" in their gymnastics class who still made the time to participate in something she loved.

BE-DO-HAVE & THE EGO

As you embark on this new path and journey of Be-Do-Have, your ego will most likely feel threatened. Remember her? She will present her reasons for you not to participate in this new venture, because you might not be safe. In the past you perhaps tried to ignore her and move forward, only to have her creep up on you in a moment of doubt, reinforcing with her relentless whispers that this was not a good idea and you were making a mistake. Now, you're going to hear her out, embrace and befriend her so that you can move forward together. First, you'll have to recognize her voice.

Here are some ways she will show up:

1. **Perfectionism:** Something else needs to be perfect before you can move forward, or you need to be sure that you can perfectly perform this new thing in order to avoid failure. Perfectionism paralyzes progress by giving you an excuse to avoid forward movement.

2. **Procrastination:** You took out the trash, fed the kids, did the dishes, and ate up all your time for the day. Tomorrow will be different. You'll start tomorrow. Hint: That to-do list refreshes every morning; there is never a convenient time to embrace change.

3. **Self-Doubt:** What if I fail? What if I embarrass myself? Remember the last time you tried this and something horrible happened? Your ego plants seeds of doubt to keep you from experiencing failure.

4. **Overwhelm:** You may find yourself thinking that there is too much to do, that you'll never be able to accomplish the tasks. The ego makes the challenge appear so huge that it prevents you from even starting. It's like looking at the top of a mountain as you attempt to climb rather than simply focusing on the next step in front of you.

5. **Fear of Judgment or Loss:** What if I am coming off as selfish? Am I changing too much? Will the people who loved me before still love me now?

Ego's voice will often feel loud and urgent. It will feel critical and judgmental. All the mistakes you've ever made will be brought to your attention. The ego will focus on the absolute worst-case scenario and all that *could* go wrong.

When you notice this voice and start feeling old patterns and stories popping up, the most powerful defense is to PAUSE.

P: Pause and acknowledge

When you feel fear, doubt, or resistance, stop and acknowledge it for what it is—the ego keeping you safe. Feel free to talk to her (out loud or in your head) from that perspective.

- Say something like, "Thank you for trying to protect me, but I am ready to choose a new way and I feel safe doing so. Let's do this together."

A: Anchor in the present moment

The ego will thrive on future what-ifs and past mishaps. When we live in the present moment, there is no fear.

- Ask yourself, what is one action I can take right now? This narrows your focus into smaller "steps" rather than the whole *mountain*.

U: Uncover false stories

Challenge the ego by asking yourself if the fear is based on fact. Or are you making an assumption?

- Recognize that most fears come from past experiences, not your current reality, and that you are creating a new story for yourself. The plot is different now. There's no need to continue to play out what happened to the previous character.

- This helps you logically separate truth from fear-based fiction and will calm the ego.

S: Step into action

Fear loses its hold on you when you take even one small action step forward.

- Choose one simple action. Whether it be a boundary, a choice, or planning a new habit or ritual. You'll notice your fear response calming as you take action.

E: Embody the feeling

Imagine and embody how it will *feel* to live as the person you want to *be*.

- Close your eyes and spend as much time as needed to visualize this new life. Do this daily, first thing in the morning or last thing before bed, as that is when our subconscious is primed. Visualize it so deeply that you start to *feel* different.
- Continue to focus on the joy and ease waiting for you on the other side; you now know the formula to get you there.

Enacting Be-Do-Have is the first step to connecting with your whole self, rejecting old models that keep you stuck, and breaking free of the constraints that your ego has built in order to keep you safe. As you continue on this path, the ego will learn that change can be good and fear isn't necessary. Your new life—and whole self—are waiting for you on the other side!

CHAPTER 5

Breaking Free

The life of the modern woman often feels like an endless carousel of to-dos and obligations: family needs, errands, work deadlines, and the effort of maintaining relationships within and outside of our homes. Somewhere in the midst of doing our best to not disappoint or lose touch with anyone else, we disappoint and lose connection with ourselves.

For too long this chaos and daily grind have been normalized. It's become the unspoken badge of honor for today's woman, the one who does it all. But chaos is not an indicator of a life well lived. It's a life spent doing our best to simply survive, get through, grab some sleep, and start it all over again the next day. Simply surviving our lives is not where our power or joy resides.

It's time to break free.

BREAKING THE CYCLE

The conditioning you have experienced isn't your fault. It's your opportunity. If you are reading this book, whether you realize it or not, you are a cycle breaker. You are someone who consciously chooses to disrupt unhealthy, harmful, and limiting elements in your life, whether generational, societal, or self-inflicted. Cycle breakers are the ones who are willing to do the inner work to heal trauma, limiting beliefs, and emotional wounds. Cycle breakers have a desire to set boundaries and crave opportunities for growth, connection, and change for themselves and future generations.

Being a cycle breaker requires courage, self-awareness, and resilience, but the rewards are profound. You free yourself from repeating old familial and societally indoctrinated patterns while stepping into a life of alignment. Even better, you're creating a new model for other women and girls. You can stand as an example in our materially driven world of someone who can *be* happy from an internal source rather than *have* happiness from external things.

The good news is that breaking the cycle doesn't require you to completely change your life overnight. It doesn't ask you to wake hours earlier to meditate, journal, or create the perfect morning routine. It doesn't require you to disappear and head to Bali for a weeklong retreat so you can "find yourself" again. Although you may feel lost, the place to truly find yourself has been *inside* you all along. You've just been focused on and distracted by everything *outside* of you—the needs, obligations, and noise of the world. You have forgotten how to hear your own voice; you have been disconnected from your whole self. Society has taught you to only love and appreciate the parts of you that perform the way a good woman would—helping others, overcommitting, and having no boundaries. Essentially, you've been tasked with being sel*fless*—literally losing your *self* for the sake of serving others.

You will find that coming home to your whole self is easier than anything you have ever tried before. You may have experienced glimpses of it in the past, moments where everything felt right, as if you were being pulled through the day rather than having to push. Anytime this happened you chalked it up to sheer luck. Recognizing that this feeling is not an anomaly but rather a deep well of resources inside of you will help you access this formula so that you can make use of it in your life whenever you want it. Going forward, you will have the choice. You can choose the old way or access the new, at any point in your life.

At times, you will choose the old way because it feels easier. Each time you do this, you will be reminded that it's not easier when that feeling of dissatisfaction blossoms again. Researchers at Cornell University determined that we make 226.7 decisions a day about food.[8] If we're making this many decisions solely on food, imagine how many decisions we make per day when it comes to everything else. Many more unconscious decisions are made automatically due to previous programming. Once you are aware of how the old cycles have permeated your decision-making—and how to consciously choose a new path—you will have an opportunity each and every time you stand at a crossroads. The choice will always be yours.

In making the new choice, you are simply returning to what has been there all along—your inner calm, your power, and your whole self. This process doesn't require or demand perfection, it just requires the courage to practice something new. Know that you will fall short at times, because remember: perfection doesn't exist! That's all part of carving a new path, breaking free, and getting to the other side where a life of more ease, calm, and joy awaits you. It truly exists.

Most importantly, breaking free isn't about fixing yourself because you were never broken. It's about remembering who you are and getting back to her, and it's easier, more natural, and more accessible than you have been led to believe. Breaking free starts with a simple shift—turning inward.

When you re-create the bond with yourself, when you come back home, something beautiful and remarkable happens. The chaos that once filled your life starts to lose its grip. You will still experience bad moments, but you will have the tools to ride the wave rather than drown in the ocean. You will stop beating up and judging yourself. You will unlock self-compassion and forgiveness. You will become the adult that you perhaps needed as a child, and you will embrace yourself in a way that you have yearned for—maybe without even fully realizing it.

The energy that keeps you stuck will soften and be replaced by a new, unshakeable calm. A calm that doesn't come from the perfect schedule or everything around you working out just right. It doesn't only show up when things are going okay with your kids or when your home is spotless. This is a calm that is created *within* and one that you can get back to time and time again in the moments when you need it most.

I'm not here to promise you something that's perfect. As you now know, that's unattainable. I am here to commit alongside you to progress and propel toward a new way. This isn't a self-help strategy. This is a movement. One that is long overdue.

It's time to regain control by breaking free.

Before we move forward, let's take a moment to pause. Have you worked through the exercises and prompts in earlier chapters? Have you noticed what has come up for you as you're going through them? At first this process may feel a bit overwhelming, and that's okay. It's new and unfamiliar, and like flexing a muscle that hasn't been used in a long time, it can feel unsteady.

Think of this process as practicing. Anytime you endure an unfamiliar situation or take a new path—whether it be creating boundaries, speaking your truth, or going after something you desire—remind yourself that you don't have to be perfect at this . . . you're *practicing*. Using that word reminds you that it will be messy and you will most likely experience some bumps along the way. Along with this thought, ditch the old myth of *practice makes perfect*—remember, perfect isn't possible. Instead, think of it as *practice builds progress*.

As you continue to practice a new workout routine, your muscles may ache, but that isn't a sign that something is wrong—quite the opposite. It's a sign of muscle growth. And while there may be temporary discomfort, I would bet it pales in comparison to the pain you have been experiencing for much of your life. This practice over time will make you stronger, more grounded, and more aligned. It will create a life of more joy, ease, and harmony.

Maybe some of these exercises have prompted you to look back on some frustrating experiences when things didn't go as planned or made you feel sadness for the way you have been showing up. But I want to remind you—it's not your fault. The overwhelm, the chaos, the stress, missing the mark, subpar relationships, not taking care of yourself—those aren't failures on your part. They're a result of unrealistic systems, expectations, and patterns that were handed down to you without your consent.

From a young age, we as women are conditioned to believe our worth is tied to how much we do for others. We're taught to be everything to everyone, to be selfless as our highest aim of being a good person. Over time the pressure grows, and we feel forced into being a wonderful mom, a supportive friend, a devoted partner, and a rockstar career woman, all while keeping a perfect home and having a great body.

Now add to that societal expectations and messages about how we shouldn't slow down. I remember a huge sign that used to hang in my gymnasium as a child that said, "If I rest,

I rust." That sign was one of the most prominent mantras that every child in that gym saw every time they trained, ingraining in them the messaging that stopping—even for a second—spelled failure. Even if that phrase isn't familiar to you, I'm sure you've heard at least one of these:

- Time is money
- I'll sleep when I'm dead
- The early bird gets the worm
- No pain, no gain
- If you're not moving forward, you're falling behind
- Winners never quit and quitters never win
- Do it right or don't do it at all

Sure, all of these have helped us have an incredible work ethic and driven athletes and performers to a higher bar. All of these reflect a way of life that generates positive outcomes but also crushes the body and spirit. I am so thankful for my drive; it has given me a successful career, taken me to heights I never thought I'd reach, and given me a sense of purpose. But when combined with the modern messaging of doing it all, it became a poison in my life. We as empowered women have let the pendulum swing too far.

Rest isn't indulgent; it's essential. Your whole self has been yearning for it, and you have heard her whispers. Connection isn't optional; it's survival. By learning to unapologetically accept restorative rest while also embracing your ability to get things done, you're not just supporting yourself, you're tapping into and connecting with the version of your whole self that can show up in the world not only for other people, but for yourself, as well.

BREAKING FREE

You picked up this book because you feel it—something is wrong. Something is off. It's because you are answering a call that your soul came here for. You are one of the women who will now break the cycles that no longer serve you, not just for yourself but for every little girl and woman who comes next. We are the new pioneers, we are the ones who may be a bit afraid but are choosing to courageously change the status quo, reclaim our wholeness, and show the world the power and beauty of our feminine connection and alignment. Most importantly, you are not doing this alone; we are all a part of something bigger than us. This is a movement of women rising together, breaking free, and creating a new way for ourselves—one that is in alignment with who we truly are, not who the world told us to be.

Every woman who picks up this book, every woman who starts practicing saying yes to herself in the big moments—and the tiny ones—and every woman that you invite to participate alongside you in this new journey becomes part of this movement. When you experience obstacles, when you feel the pull to play small, to go back to old ways, remember that you are surrounded by a collective of women who are also making the choice to step into our power. You belong here—with us. This is our community, and together we are unstoppable. You belong and you are seen—truly seen. You are worthy and deserving, and you are never alone in this.

So let's rewrite the rules. Let's make history. Let's shake things up and change the game. Let's create a world where our daughters and granddaughters can live fully, unapologetically, and powerfully in their softness. This is your moment. This is our movement.

Here we go.

Part 2

GETTING ALIGNED

CHAPTER 6

Teaming Up with Your Ego

In a society that rewards perceived feminine qualities such as politeness, perfection, and people-pleasing, it can feel rebellious to get to know, embrace, and be willing to show up as your whole self. But what if all the parts you have become an expert at hiding from the world—the messy, loud, deep, angry, bitter, imperfect versions of you—are the keys to unlocking your power?

This chapter is an invitation to shed the protective layers you have built up over your lifetime out of fear, previous rejection, or past moments of opening yourself up, only to be hurt. Rejection, critique, and negative feedback from mentors and peers alike have taught you which parts of you are acceptable and which ones aren't. The parts that others have rejected still hold value and are part of what makes you, and everyone else, human. There is a secret power inside the element of yourself that you have neglected, stifled, and otherwise stamped down in order to project an image that society has taught you is desirable, even necessary.

But an image is all it is—your whole self has yet to emerge, claim her power, and make herself known. Because we are going to be tapping into a resource that you have spent a lifetime trying to ignore, this leap can be very scary. It's simple, but that doesn't mean it's always going to be easy. Let's take a look at some of the uncomfortable feelings that may come up when you begin to have a conversation with your ego, instead of trying to shut her up.

UNLOCKING THE FREEDOM OF YOUR WHOLE SELF

For so many of us, showing up as our true self feels risky. We have been conditioned to dull our edges, dim our light, and fit into containers in the hopes that we will be accepted by others who do the same. We have become masters at blending in. We have all been there: tiptoeing into a room, scanning the energy, assessing and observing the unspoken rules.

How do they interact? What's funny to them? What engages them? Who/what do they trash talk? Without even realizing it most of the time, we begin to watch and assess the group dynamic; we do our best to tune in to the invisible frequency. Without realizing it, we adjust our energy to match it. It's as if we turn into a human radio dial, cautiously turning the knob to find the station that feels safest.

In one situation or room, we may turn up our humor and downplay our intelligence. In another, we may amplify our drive, our ambition, and our competitive nature. In almost all of them, we mute our vulnerability. It's as if we're scrolling through social media, choosing which filter to use, picking the one that fits the scene and hiding those that don't. But here's the issue with this: When we live this way, we never fully tune in to our own frequency. We don't even know what our own channel sounds like anymore.

It's a terrible thought, isn't it? The idea that you've worked so hard to fit in that you've lost yourself can be a hard concept to grasp. We think like chameleons, doing our best to blend seamlessly into the room. But we are not blending—we're disappearing. When we continue to camouflage our true colors, nobody ever truly sees us—not even ourselves. We're present in the room, but we have vanished in plain sight. We need to pull back the camouflage to find our real selves.

I'm not here to berate you for falling into line and acquiescing to cultural norms—literally everyone does that. Don't feel guilt, shame, or do any self-blaming for not knowing what your own frequency sounds like—nobody else does either. As women, we've been absorbing strong messaging for so long that it has drowned out our unique voices, and you are not alone in feeling silenced.

This desire to fit in and willingness to lose ourselves in the process isn't conscious; it's instinctual. The need to be part of a group is deeply rooted in our psychology and biology. For much of our history as humans, our survival was dependent on belonging to a community. Safety, food, and protection were collective efforts of the tightly knit tribes our ancestors relied on to continue our species. Rejection or isolation from the group wasn't just tough socially; it literally threatened their lives. This has been stamped onto our biology, a primal code in our genetics that is still felt today through FOMO, or that intense feeling you get when you come across everyone hanging out . . . but you weren't invited.

The irony of altering yourself in order to fit the room actually creates more of the one thing you are expending so much energy on trying to avoid—loneliness. Although you are surrounded by people, you feel isolated and alone because the version they like isn't really *you*. Although it may seem hard to believe, it's more painful to be loved for someone you're not than to risk rejection by being your true self. Showing up as a false, filtered, armored, or masked version of yourself creates shallow, meaningless relationships that will never be fulfilling for you. Courageously taking baby steps to deprogram yourself from a lifetime of strong messaging —as well as genetic coding—leads to and fosters more meaningful connections. What you truly desire isn't more people or more noise in your life, it's authentic connection—and the most important piece of that begins with connecting with yourself first.

There is a much greater reward in being fully seen and accepted for who you truly are than there is in maintaining a lot of shallow relationships. Even if it means your circle shrinks, the quality of the connections you make once you show up as your whole self will be so much more fulfilling. You will belong not because you assessed and matched the room, but because you presented your whole self—and attracted people who liked it!

IDENTIFYING YOUR MESSY BITS— AND ACCEPTING THEM

Your big sister ego has been working since you were a child to amass a lifetime of data on what parts of you are unacceptable. You've worked hard to sublimate, overpower, and choke out those aspects because you've learned that they are unworthy, even scary. But that doesn't mean they stopped being part of you or that they don't exist anymore. They're still there, and squashing them down only means that you're ignoring your own needs. Sure, we've all got our ugly bits that we wish weren't part of us. But—hard fact—they are. Learning how to identify what these parts are, what they say about you, and how to convert them into a useful dialogue with yourself is a key element to embracing your ego.

For example, let's say you have a bad temper. Maybe you anger easily and tend to snap at people. Maybe you keep everything bottled up, only to have it explode. Either way, I guarantee that every time you've indulged this part of yourself, there were social consequences. You might have even done the work all on your own, feeling guilt and shame, and promising yourself that you are never, *ever*, going to do that again. Well, guess what? You are. Because your temper is part of you. Instead of thinking of your temper as a bad thing, let's reframe it so that we're not using black-and-white language.

When you get angry, snap, or lose your temper, it is likely because you have an unexpressed need. Let's say you finally got 30 minutes to yourself and sat down with the library book that's due next week . . . and your daughter started practicing piano. Now? Can't she see that you're trying to relax? Isn't that incredibly selfish of her? How is it that you can't get a single moment of peace in your own home? There are two possible outcomes here—either you snap at her, damaging your relationship and making yourself feel like a crap mom—or you tell yourself that she needs to practice, and *you're* the one being selfish. So you put the book down and go find something else to do while she's playing . . . like cleaning out the fridge, because that needs to be done anyway, and it won't interrupt her.

But what's really going on is that you're having a natural human reaction to having something you need—some downtime—taken away from you by someone else. Losing your temper isn't you being a bad person, or a less-than-awesome mom. It's you being human, expressing your need . . . just not in a constructive way. If you *don't* lose your temper, you just fall back into people-pleasing mode, let others get their needs met, and keep walking around as the depleted, unfulfilled woman who serves everyone else.

Next time you're on the verge of snapping or feel your anger rising, instead of expressing the anger in a way that hurts others—or keeping it inside and hurting yourself—have a conversation with it. Investigate this shadow element of yourself that you've kept at bay for so long or been taught is unacceptable. Are you angry because you're a selfish person? Or is there a need of yours that isn't being met? Ask yourself why you're angry. What are you missing in your life that your temper flashed over this particular thing?

Chances are you'll find out that you're not a horrible, selfish, angry, inflammatory, battle-axe of a woman. You're just a human who has a need that is being denied, and you lashed out in a negative way, using up energy that is better shifted toward analyzing the anger and identifying what it is you're missing in your life.

Sitting down face-to-face with your messy bits isn't fun and can induce a lot of shame, panic, and fear. But once you've truly taken a look at the parts of yourself that you've denied for so long, you'll see that they are serving a purpose. Your job in reconnecting with your whole self is to identify what that purpose is and how you can tap into that energy in a constructive way.

Once you learn how to step into your whole self and embrace the parts of you that you've been ignoring or trying to overcome, you'll reap the benefits of living in the new way.

HOW YOUR WHOLE SELF IMPACTS OTHERS

When you step closer into your whole self, you will likely start to notice a disharmony between yourself and some of the people you have been surrounded by. Maybe the jokes don't feel as funny, or perhaps you don't like how you feel during or after your time with them, because you are no longer aligned with them. In fact, it's possible you never were and just didn't recognize it. It's okay to outgrow relationships, and there is nothing wrong with feeling the ache that comes with desiring something different or something more.

There is an inherent social risk that comes when you stop blending in and start standing in. You might lose some people. Relationships will shift and some friendships will likely fade. This is scary because our instincts tell us that these actions can threaten our survival. It can feel selfish, me-centric, and even like a betrayal. Yet, when you cling to what no longer fits or works, you betray *yourself*. You aren't leaving these people behind, you are simply stepping forward.

And here's the best part of this—it's very possible they will follow you! When you start showing up as your whole self, you give others permission to do the same. You emit an energy, a resonance that is magnetic. Your people will find you. They will see you; they will be inspired by you. The depth of connection created with these people will far surpass the bond you thought you had when you were blending in.

When you first start to carve out this space for yourself, an interesting thing might happen. The people closest to you might push back or feel threatened. This happens for one of a number of reasons. They could be afraid to lose you as you move forward. Your growth is also a subconscious reminder to them that they can do the same. If someone isn't ready to get unstuck yet, they might not be a fan of you choosing differently.

When I first started to say yes to myself more often by giving myself a few minutes in the morning for what I truly needed—quiet time, journaling, reflection, nurturing—my husband felt left out. I could feel his energy and even his behavior shift; he was like a kid doing anything to get your attention, while never actually knowing what he wanted. Finally, after months of him feeling this frustration with me, he had a bit of an explosion, and it all came out.

"You're completely ignoring me in the morning," he said. "You don't even talk to me anymore." I was so glad he finally shared what had been on his heart. I needed to hear it in his words so we could work through it together. I needed to give him space to get to the bottom of what was bothering him so we could connect on it and figure out our new way. It also gave me a chance to show him that I had lost myself—in the busyness of raising a family, our work, our lives—I had completely lost touch with who I was. If only for a few moments, while the world was asleep, I desperately needed to get back to her, to that version of me that I didn't even know anymore.

I told him I didn't like how I was showing up for him or the kids anymore, and it stemmed from not showing up for myself. I assured him I was still *with* him, and we just needed to figure out other ways for us to connect. Had I let his needs interfere with my own, I would have dropped this me-time, and our relationship would have suffered more in the long run. I would have yet again put myself and my needs at the bottom. On the surface, he and I would have been connecting. He may have even thought all was well, but deep down my anger, resentment, and frustration would have kept growing—not good ingredients for the healthy marriage I was looking to co-create with him.

We promised to start carving out weekly date nights when possible. He also told me that he wanted to feel connected in the morning and wanted to be close, to physically touch. I maintained my boundaries; I spoke up for what I needed and craved, and on the other side of that, we unlocked the next level of our relationship. Now he will often join me by putting his head on my lap while I'm in meditation or reading my book in the morning. I am so glad that I realized I was worthy of this time for myself, and that he came to see it as well. It was not only that I needed and deserved it. It would make me stronger and healthier while doing the same for my relationship with my husband. Standing in and speaking up for what I needed made all the difference.

THE REWARD OF STANDING IN YOUR WHOLE SELF

Belonging isn't about fitting in; it's about getting reconnected with your whole self and courageously standing in your power from that place. Showing up in rooms and asking yourself what it is that you want from the experience will bring you energy. When you do your best to assume what everyone else wants or needs, and then morph yourself into that version, it is draining. If you've ever felt like you have to put on a costume or pretend to be someone else from the moment you wake up in the morning to when you fall asleep, you have not been in touch with your true self. This realization is a powerful moment. It's a pull rather than a push once you finally understand it and are ready to embrace it. And the benefits you reap on the other side are well worth the journey.

Living Authentically: You will no longer be filtered or confined by your view of societal expectations on your life. You will confidently express your thoughts and emotions genuinely. Showing up this way fosters deeper, more meaningful relationships as others are drawn to your sincerity and open energy.

Inner Peace: This feeling will emanate from a place of understanding your desires, and decision-making will become clearer and more straightforward. This clarity reduces inner conflict and tension, leading to a calmer, tranquil mind and heart.

Enhanced Well-Being: Aligning with yourself positively impacts your mental and physical health. Studies show that self-acceptance can lead to overall improved emotional well-being and reduced stress.

Sense of Purpose: Getting to know yourself and aligning with yourself provides a sense of purpose and satisfaction. Each day starts to feel more meaningful, as though you are living for something greater than yourself. This keeps daily stressors in perspective and broadens our focus outside of us.

Growth and Inner Resilience: Embracing your whole self allows you to integrate and love all parts of yourself—even those messy bits. This concept of self-acceptance fosters resilience, allowing you to navigate life's challenges more easily.

WHY THIS TIME IS DIFFERENT

You may be reading this and feeling a bit of overwhelm or that familiar defeated feeling you've felt before. You've gotten so excited about the potential of a new way in the past and then hit this crossroads. The oh-so-familiar place you've been anytime you've read a self-help book or heard about a new fad diet that will actually help you shed the weight this time . . . only to have reality set in. This won't work for you because the system they need you to follow isn't realistic for your life.

Know that this time truly is different. I want to meet you at the place of overwhelm where you are about to be presented with the work of the new way and assure you as a busy woman that *this* is finally the way that will work. It's so much easier than you think, and you are not doing it alone this time.

Are you someone who is thinking *I don't even know where to start. Who am I? What do I even want? What do I even like?* That's completely natural, and you're not alone. So many of us feel this way after decades of focusing all our efforts on everything and everyone outside of ourselves. The beautiful thing about this process and the whole Connection Code is that it isn't about becoming something new; this isn't an addition—it's a subtraction, a letting go, a coming home. And we're doing this together.

EXERCISES AND PRACTICES

1. What emotions am I feeling most often right now? Are there any that I have been suppressing or avoiding?

2. When I feel [insert emotion], what physical sensations show up in my body? Where do I notice heaviness or discomfort?

3. What stories do I tell myself (or hear my big sister ego telling me) about my less attractive qualities? What could happen if I fully express these emotions?

4. Is the worst-case scenario of what could happen from expressing these emotions true?

5. What situations or people tend to trigger my strongest emotions?
6. If this emotion could speak, what would it say? What is it trying to tell me?

REFRAMING

1. What is one negative emotion I feel often? How might this emotion be tied to or a sign of something I care deeply about?
2. What is this emotion helping me realize I want more of in my life?
3. What strengths does this emotion point to? If I could rename this emotion as a gift or superpower, what would I call it and why?
4. What lesson has this emotion taught me, or what experience has this emotion protected me from in the past? How did it help me grow and set boundaries?

EXAMPLES OF REFRAMING NEGATIVE EMOTIONS

Jealousy: What am I jealous of right now? What does this tell me about what I desire? How can I take a step toward creating a version of this in my life?

Sadness: What does sadness want me to slow down and take notice of?

Fear: What fear is holding me back? What might it be trying to protect me from, and how can I honor it while still taking a step forward?

DISCOVERING YOUR POWER

1. What is the main emotion I have judged myself for? How can I show empathy and compassion to myself for feeling this way? How can I create space to feel and learn from this emotion?

2. If I were to use this emotion as a guide, what action would propel me closer to alignment with my whole self? Example: If resentment is telling me I have taken on too much, how can I use it to ask for help?

3. If I thanked this emotion for its presence in my life, what would I say?

EMPOWERMENT

1. What stories have I been telling myself about my emotions? How can I rewrite these stories in order to reflect my strength and resilience?

2. What emotions or parts of myself have I judged in the past? Can I embrace them as I move into wholeness?

3. What would it feel like to view all my emotions and parts of myself as teammates on my journey to self-discovery?

4. How can I listen to and honor my emotions without being controlled or limited by them?

CHAPTER 7

Gifts of the Ego

Thank god for your ego.

I'm guessing that's not a phrase you've heard very often. We've all been taught that our ego is primarily a negative thing, something that enhances our less-than-desirable qualities like self-importance, or accentuates a harmful drive, such as greed or pride. The truth is that the old model of the ego is outdated and, incidentally, is a great tool for making women feel guilt or shame . . . like we need another dose of those in our lives. Now that you have reframed your ego not as something that you should be working against, but rather with, let's explore the positive qualities that your ego can bring into your life—they really do exist!

We've talked about how the ego is your overprotective big sister, the one who has been taking notes since you were a kid and saw all the times you experienced pushback, rejection, and outright failure. She's there to remind you of those moments when you consider trying something new; she's there to keep you still, small, and stuck. This all sounds negative and like the ego is something to be overcome, doesn't it?

Truth bomb—it's not.

In keeping you safe, the ego is essentially stepping in as an aspect of survival, because the ego knows a secret—you're special. You're unique. You're the only person who can show up as *you* throughout the entire history of the universe. As a result, the ego wants to make sure you are preserved, that the specialness that is *you* continues to exist. The magic of the Connection Code is that once you have partnered with your ego instead of trying to silence her, you're not the only one who experiences a transformation—your big sister ego does, too! And when you do so, you inspire others to do the same.

When your ego learns that all of those special, unique, quirky little bits shouldn't be silenced, but rather accentuated and looked upon as strengths, she reframes her position. She'll turn all of that negative energy that was holding you back into a propelling force that will guide you forward. The difference? The next time you're in a business meeting and you have a point to make, your ego will say—*hell, yeah, speak your original, authentic piece, sis!* Rather than—*hey, remember that other time you spoke up and were dismissed because your ideas were too off the wall? Let's avoid that and be quiet.* Befriending the ego means that she is converted from the worried, overprotective big sister to your biggest cheerleader, the voice that encourages you to step up, stand in, and be seen!

GIFTS OF THE EGO

The cheerleader and the big sister won't switch places overnight, and they won't wholly drown out each other either. The two of them will go back and forth, creating a tug-of-war inside your mind that may create conflict, but ultimately provides growth. Befriending the ego and allowing her to develop into her whole self—protector and cheerleader—means that you will be able to reap the benefits described on the next page.

Self-Protection & Survival

- The ego construct serves to keep us safe in a world that can feel unpredictable and threatening. The ego's ability to create boundaries and alert us to perceived threats ensures our survival by helping us avoid dangerous situations and protects our physical and emotional well-being.

Sense of Identity & Individuality

- The ego is responsible for us forming a sense of self unique from others. This allows us to know our strengths, values, and preferences, and enables self-expression.
- Ego allows us to assert ourselves and come from a place of defined boundaries and self-awareness.

Motivation & Achievement

- Ego is what drives us. Thanks to our ego, we seek accomplishment, growth, and recognition. When accessed from a healthy place, this desire can propel us into forward momentum, helping us pursue and achieve our goals, take risks, and experience personal growth.

Self-Discovery

- The contrast between the yin and yang of ego and our true self creates a duality that opens the door to self-discovery. Without the contrast of the fears, judgments, and insecurities of the ego, we wouldn't fully experience the qualities of our true self—peace, calm, compassion, and intuition. This polarity helps us appreciate both aspects of ourselves and can foster growth toward balance and wholeness.

Connection and Empathy Through Shared Struggle

- The struggles and challenges created by our ego—fear, insecurity, self-judgment—are part of the human experience. Recognizing these aspects in ourselves helps us empathize with others, knowing everyone faces their own inner battle. This authentic experience has the ability to create deep connections as we recognize our shared humanity and support one another on this path to self-acceptance through authenticity and vulnerability.

Catalyst for Growth & Inner Work

- The ego is a mirror, reflecting the parts of us that need attention, healing, support, and compassion. By listening to the ego, we have the ability to evolve toward our whole selves and deepen our self-awareness.

- The ego is not an enemy. Integration of the ego and true self contributes to a balanced life. This whole self emerges compassionate, yet aware of the importance of boundaries. Curious, yet assured. Embracing the ego rather than suppressing it creates a harmonious relationship where we can honor both its strengths and limitations, leading us to a deeper connection with ourselves and others.

When we befriend the ego, these traits become the greatest gifts and a source for some of our most empowering qualities.

SETTING BOUNDARIES

Have you ever felt taken advantage of? Whether at work, in your relationships, or maybe even at home? Perhaps there has been a time at work when you felt overwhelmed because your boss kept adding projects onto your plate. The ego might have started whispering (or even internally screaming) *This isn't fair! I can't keep up!* This frustration isn't bad; it's a sign that a boundary has been crossed.

Maybe this shows up in your home, as mentioned before, when you strike out in irritation at your children when you are doing something important to you—be it work or leisure—and are constantly interrupted. Most likely, when you finally get to put your head on the pillow, you will self-talk through all the ways you are messing up your kids and how much therapy they'll need. Ever happen to you? Just me?!

It can show up in your friendships, too. Are you the friend that everyone goes to for help or calls to dump on? Are you the one always saying yes to them and no to yourself? If so, your ego may trigger exhaustion, resentment, avoidance, bitterness, or anger. Then your mind runs with the narrative, remembering and tabulating all the times your friends have been takers rather than givers. You play it out during your commute, thinking of how you're going to show up and what you're going to say the next time a friend puts you in that position. But when the moment arises again, fear shows up and you allow your boundaries to be crossed once again, because you don't want to be perceived as selfish or lose a friend or someone close to you. This is where most people cave, missing the magic of tuning in to the gifts of the ego.

When you can start to establish a habit of tuning in and listening to these intense feelings and alarms from the ego, you can ask what it is here to tell us. Creating space to do so is essential, and we'll walk through that together shortly. The ego in its healthy state gives you the courage to say, "I matter too." Your ego allows you to finally put yourself first, not because you don't care about others, but because you're finally starting to recognize that you matter just as much as they do. The ego gives you the pull you need to stand firm and to preserve yourself, even when it feels uncomfortable.

COURAGE

Ego allows you to be brave enough to step into hard conversations and face your fears head-on. We often think of courage as a heart-centered quality, but the truth is courage is born out of your ego's instinct for self-preservation, protection, and survival. The true self encourages us to grow and expand; it's actually the ego that finally gives us the push we need in order to act. Courage doesn't happen in the absence of fear—it's action in the presence of fear—and fear is ego's home turf. Fear is where the ego shines.

One of the ego's most important and strongest qualities is its desire to avoid pain and discomfort. In much of our life we choose to stay stuck in subpar situations, jobs, or relationships because of our fear of the unknown. The ego's strong desire to avoid pain and discomfort (though it sometimes leads to avoidance behaviors) can actually work in our favor. The ego is the one that eventually realizes that staying the same is actually more painful than facing the unknown. When you have finally hit that limit, and the ego says, "I've had enough," you experience a catalyst for change.

Maybe you've been in a toxic work environment for far too long. Whether it's your boss, co-workers, or just the workload that upsets and triggers you, the ego will finally say, "I can't do this anymore!" Miraculously, the pain and discomfort of staying outweigh the fear of leaving. This push eventually drives you to have the tough conversations and make the decisions necessary for next steps.

Let's take a look at how this might show up in a relationship. Maybe you have been tolerating a partnership or friendship that has been incredibly one-sided. You show up for him/her but he/she rarely—if ever—reciprocates. One day, your ego blurts out, "Enough!" This moment of jarring clarity and finality gives you the courage to turn your back or, better yet, speak out and say, "I love you, but I also love myself, and this isn't working anymore."

If you feel like you have hit your breaking point and just can't go on like this anymore, that is the pivotal moment where the ego is pushing you to act. The pain of staying stuck now outweighs the fear of breaking free.

TAKING UP SPACE

The cheerleader ego says, "I am here and I matter!" The ego doesn't want to blend in or stay invisible—although we often do. The ego craves individuality and a unique identity. The ego is what's responsible for people choosing to step into visibility, take up space, and fully be seen—even when at first it may feel terrifying.

What self-shrinking behaviors and beliefs have we let speak over this aspect of the ego? For many women—especially middle-aged women—there is a belief that you need to be easy, agreeable, and likable. Youth and (according to society) beauty are leaving you, so you need to ensure that you are still an acceptable person by being nice. This might look like staying quiet in meetings when you have a good idea begging to be heard or when you disagree with an idea and know there is a better solution. When the cheerleader aspect of the ego finally chimes in, reminding you that your voice deserves to be heard, you speak up . . . and discover that your idea was exactly what the team needed.

Perhaps you're contemplating or feeling called toward a career or life transition, or starting a new passion project. At first, you may be fearful of the newness, the unknown, but eventually the fear can turn into an "I'm meant for more" mantra. That's your ego giving you the courage to step up and be fully seen.

Courage doesn't always look or feel like a bold or brave moment. It can also be quiet, steady, and focused. Courage is the decision to take up space, value your presence, and know your worth.

ADVOCATE FOR YOURSELF AND OTHERS

Your ego is a natural advocate, always defending what it cares about—including your loved ones. The ego says, "This isn't okay." This internal message becomes a powerful force of action, empowering you to speak up for yourself and others. This may mean speaking up for fair treatment or pay in a career, standing up for your kids, or speaking your truth in relationships—being clear what your needs are and that they deserve to be met. Many of us have been conditioned to hold our voice in for the sake of being "agreeable," but ego's protective nature will pull us forward, allowing us to stand firm.

Perhaps at work someone interrupts you mid-sentence in a meeting, presentation, or conversation. You may hear a voice urging you to remain calm, but your ego chimes in, telling you that you have every right to speak out. You calmly but firmly say, "I'd like to finish my thoughts before you share yours."

Maybe your child's teacher makes a dismissive comment about their learning style. While you aim to avoid uncomfortable confrontation, the ego reminds you, "this is important," inspiring you to boldly and powerfully speak up for your kiddo.

In the realm of friendships, perhaps you have historically been the go-to person for a friend in need, but it's starting to really take a toll on you. Next time your friend reaches out and you feel spread thin but obliged to help out, ego steps in and says, "Your well-being matters too." You tell your friend clearly, kindly, and directly that you can't help her this time.

Advocating for yourself doesn't have to feel like a fight. It can simply be a clear and direct assertion of your needs. The ego gives you the courage to do so without guilt or the need to apologize.

BREAK CYCLES AND IGNITE CHANGE

This is one of the biggest gifts (and my personal favorite) of the ego. While the true self invites us into growth, it's the ego that says, "I refuse to live this way anymore." The ego is what pushes us to break cycles of generational patterns, toxic relationships, or self-sabotaging aspects of our lifestyle. Breaking cycles and making changes takes enormous courage because it often requires going against social norms, family traditions, and deeply ingrained beliefs. The ego finally realizes that staying in this cycle is no longer safe. The fight response of the ego is the aspect responsible for finally breaking free and starting a new path, not just for you, but for all the women who come next.

This can take the form of breaking toxic generational cycles. Did you grow up in a home where nobody talked about or felt safe fully expressing their emotions? Your cheerleader ego gives you the courage to break that cycle for your own kids by normalizing feelings and expressing and discussing emotions—even the complicated, messy ones. In a toxic relationship, you may have tolerated your partner's behavior for years because making changes or leaving felt scarier than staying. Your ego has had enough; the fear of the unknown becomes less intimidating than staying, and you break free. Or perhaps you have a habit of starting projects or new health practices but never see them through. Your ego becomes fed up with letting yourself down and decides to push through and persevere this time.

Cycle breaking isn't just courageous—it's revolutionary. It not only enhances your life, but all the lives around you. Your ego is the inner advocate that finally ignites that fire and takes action in these bold moves.

WHEN EGO AND TRUE SELF FORM A DEEP FRIENDSHIP, A COURAGEOUS WOMAN EMERGES

This woman speaks her truth without apologizing. She sets boundaries without guilt (gift of ego) but explains those boundaries with compassion and love (gift of true self). This woman ends toxic cycles in her family, partnerships, and relationships with firm resolve (ego), while also displaying grace and patience for those who are still living in the cycle (true self). Messages from the ego are the push you often need in order to take action. This is the power of integrating the ego and true self.

For so long, you've been living a fragmented life. You've blamed yourself for not fully showing up, for falling short of the life you know you deserve. But how could you have shown up fully when you were working with only 50 percent of your power? The old approach has left you disconnected from a vital part of yourself—the part that fights, speaks up, and drives you to face discomfort head-on. Without it, you've been stuck in a loop of self-doubt, over-giving, and never quite feeling like you're enough.

You are enough. You always have been. You were never broken. You were just operating with half of your potential. This shift—this reclamation of your wholeness—is where your true power lies. Now you're not just showing up with the softness and wisdom of your true self, you're also bringing in the courage, boundaries, and assertiveness of your ego. Together, they create a force that is unstoppable.

No longer will you blend in to feel safe. No longer will you shrink to keep the peace. No longer will you abandon yourself to meet the expectations of others. From here on out, you're showing up as a whole, integrated being. You're standing in your power, not blending into the background. When you live from the gifts of your true self and your ego, you become a powerful and loving force. A woman who knows how to hold compassion without self-sacrifice. A woman who can lead with an open heart and a strong voice.

Recently, our eight-year-old daughter was gearing up to perform at the halftime show at the Miami Heat basketball arena. As the day of the performance approached, fear started to kick in. We all know it. That voice inside you that creeps up and tells you all the worst-case things that could happen. Remember—our ego protects our identity, so these reminders often point to you making a fool out of yourself.

I walked Kaia through partnering with her ego just as I do with mine. When I asked her what the voice in her head was telling her, she responded that she was afraid she would fall on her head when she did a back walkover. I asked her what would help her feel better. She sat for a moment and realized that it was the wooden floor of the basketball court itself that was frightening her, having only practiced on grass turf. That afternoon, she and her dad worked through practicing back walkovers on the wooden floor in our home. When it came time for the performance, I was holding my breath, just praying all would go well. Then, there was my daughter, featured front and center on the huge Jumbotron right at the very beginning of the halftime show. I watched her nail it, and I saw her face when she did. I could tell the moment she felt that incredible feeling of accomplishment when she came out on the other side, all because she tuned in and partnered up with what her ego was telling her.

This is what alignment looks like. Not perfection. Not a polished version of you that never makes mistakes. Alignment is a life lived with your whole self—your light, your shadows, your gifts, your edges. It's bringing every part of you to the table and knowing you belong there. You've always been powerful, but now you're unstoppable. Because now, you know how to wield every part of who you are. No more hiding. No more apologizing for taking up space. You were made for this. The world doesn't need more people blending in. It needs more women like you—fully seen, fully whole, and fully aligned. This is your return to power. Your comeback. Your homecoming. And you're already on your way.

> ### REFLECTIVE QUESTIONS & PRACTICES
>
> #### Reframe Your Ego:
>
> - Think of a time recently or in the past when your ego used fear to hold you back by pointing out worst-case scenarios or past failures. How could you reframe these messages as an act of protection rather than a reason to stay stuck or play small?
>
> - Journal Prompt: In what ways has my ego been trying to keep me safe? How can I reframe these moments as acts of love from my overprotective big sister?
>
> #### Uncover Ego's Gifts:
>
> - Write down three times in your life where ego has helped you set boundaries, advocate for yourself, or find courage. How did these experiences impact you?
>
> #### Build a Relationship with Your Ego:
>
> - Next time her voice shows up, practice a dialogue with your ego. Ask it what it is trying to protect you from and have a convo on how you can work together. Ask her what she needs to feel safe so that you can move forward and grow together, while also being sure you are aware of any potential risks and that you're coming at the situation as prepared for success as possible.
>
> - Reflect on a recent time when you felt conflicted between playing small or staying stuck and stepping forward into your power. What was ego's role in that moment, and how did she help or hinder you?

- Journal Prompt: When I feel stuck between fear and courage, what is my ego protecting me from, and how can we work together on moving forward?

Boundaries:

- Identify at least one area in your life where you have struggled to set boundaries. In those situations, what has ego been trying to protect you from? What is a small step you can take in honoring yourself in this area?

- Think of a moment where you had the courage to face a difficult challenge or growth opportunity. What role did ego play in helping you find the courage to face it?

Taking Up Space:

- Identify at least one area in your life where you might be shrinking or staying quiet to blend in. What would it look/feel like to step into your power in those situations?

- How can you let your ego cheerleader help you take up space and fully show up?

Breaking Free:

- Identify one pattern, habit, behavior, or relationship you are ready to break free from. How is your ego signaling it's time for change? How can you partner with your ego in order to break free and create something new?

CHAPTER 8

The Connection Code

Imagine this: You're standing in the middle of chaos—relatives are fighting, work tasks and e-mails are piling up, dinner is burning on the stove—and you feel that oh-so-familiar sense of overwhelm creeping in. Or maybe you're sitting alone and the quiet is so heavy it feels too scary to navigate on your own. Maybe you've hit a break where you don't have anything to do . . . and now you don't know what to do with yourself. How do you handle those moments? How do you find your center, your strength, your alignment, your *connection*?

This chapter is your road map to changing your life by making different guided choices in those moments, exactly when you need them. Not in the hour of me-time that you programmed into the early morning while everyone else was asleep or the 30 minutes you get to yourself in the bathtub. There's a version of your life full of moments where you choose yourself, where you listen to the whisper of your inner voice saying *I can't do this right now*. This is about knowing what you need and accessing it when you need it most.

WELCOME TO YOUR CONNECTION CODE

By now, you're likely recognizing your own power and realizing that the journey back to your true self is more about remembering than discovering something entirely new. It's as if you're rediscovering yourself, realizing you've been there all along, just hidden beneath layers and layers that have accumulated over the years. These layers could have formed as shields against past traumas, preventing your true self from feeling safe enough to emerge, or perhaps due to fatigue, imbalances, or other reasons.

The crux lies in understanding that you're inherently and divinely connected to yourself, and our task together is simply to guide you back to that place. Your birthright is alignment, ease, and connection in your body, mind, and soul. You're here to embody your highest self fully, and as we dwell more in that state, nature's clues will lead us onward along the path of alignment, enlightenment, and our own truths. Yet, the reality is, throughout life, we all stray from alignment from time to time. Some may even feel constantly out of sync. How do you discern when you're aligned versus not?

RECOGNIZING WHEN YOU'RE OUT OF ALIGNMENT

Do you ever have those days where everyone and everything seems to get under your skin? Where the heavy breather next to you in yoga class is enough to make you leave early? Or when the sounds of the person next to you chewing their food are like nails on a chalkboard? Perhaps you grabbed the crappy shopping cart . . . again. You know the one. You try to pull it out of the corral, but it's stuck to the one in front of it. You try to keep it casual and gently tug again, only to realize it's *still* stuck, and you end up shaking the entire line of carts with your manic energy, looking slightly off-kilter.

Or maybe you are a busy mom, and in those moments where you are juggling dinner, work e-mails, and kids' homework, and feeling exhausted, you beat yourself up. You know you need to be in the fully competent and ticking-off-boxes mode, but you also want to turn all that off at the moment. Your sweet child needs you, and you don't want to be annoyed at them for breaking your flow. Your brain is urging you to get sh*t done, but your heart is telling you to sit down, chill out, and connect with your kid.

Perhaps you have been doing it all—and I do mean *all* of it. You're ahead of schedule, the house is in order, you hit the gym earlier today, dinner is on the table. You are killing it. Then, out of nowhere, life happens. Something BIG or little happens that just throws your whole vibe. You're moving quickly through the day, perhaps constantly focused on what's next rather than being in the moment, and boom, in one swift move as you reach for something, you knock over your glass of water. But it doesn't just spill, it shatters all over the counter, dripping down through the drawers, and there are now shards of invisible glass all over your kitchen floor—the room you tend to be barefoot in much of the time. In a tizzy, while you are cleaning it up, you decide to put something back in the fridge, and out flies a tub of something liquidy enough to ooze itself all over the glass-laden floor. Perhaps it's that quart of freshly whipped cream you were going to indulge in later in the form of whipped-cream-topped strawberries. Not anymore. Your plans for a decadent dessert are ruined ... and so is your entire day.

This one small water spill just derailed it all, reminding you that the perfection you aimed for is futile, and you can't have nice things. You shut down and tune out, focusing on that one bad thing that supersedes all the good in your day. You've been burning the candle at both ends, pushing away the signals your body has been giving you that a break is needed—even if you are succeeding at all the things. You ignored that whisper at your own peril, and now you're in the middle of a breakdown.

These are your signals. This is how you know you are out of alignment. Ideally, after reading this book, these things happen fewer times, plus you are going to know how to get yourself back on the train when they do. When you have the squeaky cart, a broken glass, or feel the push-pull of the work-family balance, you'll immediately recognize what's happening and know exactly what to do.

Recognizing When You're In Alignment

So now that we have discussed the way many of us have spent most of our lives in overwhelm, stress, and disconnection, let's cover what alignment feels like. How do we know when we're in it? More importantly, how do we create it?

When you are in alignment, you will feel light, free, happy, joyful. You just know it's a good day. Maybe the music is hitting just right. Perhaps as an extra bonus, you're having a really great hair day. Everything is happening easily, and somehow you're getting it all done. You feel like a rockstar. It's like someone has your back, and you are being easily pulled through life, rather than pushing your way through as if you are behind a giant boulder. You're seamlessly able to pivot in the moment between work mode and mama mode. You can be working on e-mails at your computer and are also able to be fully present when your kiddo saunters up to you with their needs.

The reason it *feels like* you are being supported and pulled through is because *you are*. You are sitting in the seat of connection with your true self—and when we do that, we are rewarded. We are here for the human experience of figuring out our purpose, our calling. We get closer to stepping into that by showing up as our highest self. When we spend more and more time in connection to our true self, we are rewarded with the feeling of flow. Think of it as angel breadcrumbs, synchronicities showing you the path, leading you along the way.

The big question is, how do we spend more time in alignment? How do we get to that place easily and seamlessly amid the busyness of our lives? Is there an accurate road map? Can we know with 100 percent certainty that the things we are putting our attention and intention into can help us experience more joy, ease, and harmony?

Yes, there is. It's called the Connection Code, and it will allow you to nourish your soul with a few minutes of intentional engagement. The Connection Code is what guides us back. The Connection Code includes ways to rediscover yourself, each of which can be accomplished within minutes, sometimes even seconds. When you have those fleeting moments here and there, these practices help nurture your being. It's about being intentional with your needs, desires, and cravings, rather than perpetually serving others or fulfilling should-dos at the expense of your wants. It's about knowing your boundaries and having the confidence to defend them. It's about giving yourself grace and permission to pause, stop, and breathe, and allowing yourself space to reconnect.

The Connection Code will help you rediscover what evokes that sensation of alignment and will prompt you to incorporate more of it into your daily routine. Now, let's delve into it.

> Proceed to the Resources page, and download the printable Connection Code at https://www.drmelissasonners.com/resources/connection-code.
>
>

We'll walk through the process together to fully grasp how transformative this can be, reshaping your life and restoring a sense of calm, ease, and equilibrium. You'll explore options for each category: Connecting with Your Body, Connecting with Your Heart, Connecting with a New Skill, and Connecting with the Divine.

After reviewing each category here and watching the corresponding video, you'll select options that resonate with you from each. These can be quick activities that take no more than a few minutes and can be seamlessly woven into the busiest of schedules, leaving you feeling more authentically yourself throughout the day and at its close. Within each category, you might also feel compelled to include activities that may not be feasible during hectic days but offer substantial emotional returns. These can be earmarked for when you can carve out more time on weekends or holidays.

This is an excellent exercise to undertake with a friend. There's immense power in having an accountability partner. An accountability partner helps us stay on point because someone else is in it with us, cheering us along the way. When you are having a down moment or need support, your partner will most likely be having an up moment, and you can lean on each other and help motivate each other through these tactics. So, grab your favorite person, share what you are doing, and embark on this journey together. Let's dive in.

CONNECTING WITH YOUR BODY

This step entails stepping out of our "monkey minds." According to research conducted by psychologists Matthew A. Killingsworth and Daniel T. Gilbert at Harvard University, the average person spends nearly 47 percent of their waking hours thinking about something other than what they're currently doing.[9] This study, which involved over 2,000 participants, used a smartphone app to track individuals' thoughts, feelings, and activities in real-time. The findings highlight the prevalence of mind-wandering and the challenge of staying fully present in the moment amid the distractions of daily life.

Many of us have too many inputs battling for our time and energy. Most of our daily thoughts are preoccupied with fretting over the past or worrying about the future. Consider your drive in the car—do you truly focus on the act of driving, or are your thoughts scattered elsewhere? Are you thinking about how to hit your benchmarks at work, or what needs to be done after that, as soon as you get home? Maybe you're even remembering that crappy comment from your friend or family member at dinner a week ago . . . but you haven't moved past it yet.

Getting into our bodies involves halting this perpetual mental chatter and immersing ourselves in the present moment or flow. It can entail dancing, exercising, moving, taking a walk, and more. In all these categories, remember to have fun, be creative, and perhaps a touch silly. Let's loosen up a bit, shall we? Personally, working mostly from home, one of my favorite ways to break the monotony is to lock the doors, don my fun belly-dancing skirt, blast Shakira's "Hips Don't Lie," and let loose! The Connection Code is about making minutes feel like hours because these activities revive our zest for life. This is how we care for ourselves in the real world, how we stave off burnout—by creating daily moments where we reconnect with our happiness, passion, and clarity.

CONNECTING WITH YOUR HEART

You know those days when you eagerly anticipate unwinding at day's end? You hustle through your tasks all day just to savor that fleeting moment of relaxation. Connecting with your heart is about creating that sanctuary within your day, even if for just a few fleeting moments. Nurturing ourselves throughout the day is paramount. My preferred method of midday nurturing involves shutting down the computer and sinking into a cozy spot while savoring a warm beverage. Whether it's lounging with a tea on the couch at home or stealing a moment of solitude while out and about, the crucial rule is to disconnect from the digital world.

This could mean losing yourself in a few pages of a book or relishing a moment of touch, perhaps with a massage chair or a brief foot massage. Connecting with our hearts is all about being as passive as possible and receiving. If I am in the midst of a very hectic day and am craving heart time, I will simply create a reframe in my intention for the day. This may mean I'm simply pivoting from talking to more of a listening role. It definitely means that I will gladly accept when someone offers to hold the door. It means I will put my hand on my heart as often as possible throughout the day and say *thank you* . . . reminding myself how often throughout this day I was able to receive. When the cashier hands me change—*thank you*. When someone compliments my shirt—*thank you*. The power of a reframe in our intention is one of the simplest ways to connect to our hearts amid the reality of our busy lives.

CONNECTING TO THE WORLD

The potency of nature cannot be overstated. Just five minutes in the fresh air can reset our entire nervous system. Once again, this step is most effective when we sever ties with digital devices. Take a stroll, hop on a bike, or simply sit beneath a tree—anything that brings you outdoors helps reestablish that connection. So step outside, even if just for a brief interlude. Nature has a knack for reminding us of the vastness of the world, pulling us out of our heads and into the present moment.

Getting into nature doesn't just feel good, it literally has a direct impact on regulating our nervous system. Spending time in natural environments has been shown to lower levels of cortisol, the primary stress hormone. The sights, sounds, and smells of nature trigger the parasympathetic nervous system, also known as the "rest and digest" response, which counteracts the stress response. The great outdoors also boosts positive psychological effects. The beauty and tranquility of natural settings evoke positive emotions such as awe, wonder, and serenity. These emotions have been linked to increased activity in brain regions associated with emotional regulation and well-being, contributing to a sense of calm and balance.

Like us, nature operates on rhythmic cycles. Similar to our circadian rhythm, nature has ebbs and flows that promote harmony and balance within the ecosystem. Something as simple as spending a few minutes in morning and evening sunlight has been shown to dramatically impact our ability to create both melatonin and serotonin, and enhance our sleep. Cycle syncing with nature promotes a feeling of harmony in our nervous system.

Direct contact with the earth, lately termed "grounding" or "earthing," has been shown to discharge excess electrical charge from the body, literally promoting stability and connectedness.

Nature also provides a rich sensory environment that, when we allow ourselves to tap into with simple prompts like, *What do I see? What do I hear? What do I smell?*, we can achieve instantaneous mindfulness and be gifted by the dissolution of time that occurs when we sit in the present moment. Nature also provides a space for introspection and self-discovery. Whether it's a solitary walk in the woods or a quiet moment on a park bench, nature invites us to ponder life's deeper questions and gain insight into ourselves.

Lastly, nature stimulates our creativity and sparks inspiration, offering a boundless source of beauty, wonder, and awe. Whether it's the vibrant colors of a sunset, the intricate patterns of a leaf, or the majestic grandeur of a mountain range, nature ignites our imagination and fuels our creative spirit.

CONNECTING WITH A NEW SKILL

When was the last time you did something new? In the digital age, we can access YouTube and learn anything we want! Although there is so much knowledge and skill we can obtain online, ideally learning a new skill is about actually engaging in it in the physical world. As with all aspects of the Connection Code, the more fun and playful you get, the better. Although learning the new skill may take some time and perhaps involve a larger commitment, such as an hour a week in a class, engaging in it and practicing it daily can take mere minutes. So why not get after it?

Maybe you've heard about everyone playing and loving pickleball and are curious but haven't taken action. This is your excuse to sign up for that pickleball clinic you keep seeing mentioned. Have you always wanted to belly dance? I know, I know, it sounds crazy, but have you always been a little bit intrigued by how those women get their bodies to move that way? I bet if you do a little research, you can find a class near you. Grab a friend, sign up, and get silly!

Learning a new skill rewards us in a few ways. It builds our self-confidence and self-esteem. Trying and succeeding at something new helps promote new neural pathways, making it easier and easier to do each time we try it. Witnessing ourselves improve at something we put our minds to can provide an instant boost to our stale routines and super full, yet annoyingly predictable lives.

It also gets us into the present time. Oh, the gift of being in the moment! How many things do you currently do while multitasking? Composing an e-mail in your head while cleaning up the dishes? Mentally compiling the grocery list when you sit down to write that e-mail? We rarely spend time in the present moment, and doing so is one of the best ways to help us feel calm and connected to ourselves. When we are engaging in something new, we have no choice but to give it our full attention.

I recently decided to join in with my kids at the skateboard park, rather than sitting on a bench and composing an e-mail. While wearing every bit of protective gear you can think of, the thought of landing on concrete was still terrifying. You can bet that every muscle and brain cell was dedicated to me not getting hurt while trying something new. I was completely, undeniably present in the moment the entire time and felt so refreshed afterward.

CONNECTING WITH THE DIVINE

Whether you've cultivated a deep connection with a higher power throughout your life or not, this step serves to tether you to something larger than yourself. It's a reminder that you're not separate from this entity, whatever form it takes for you. For some, this might involve engaging in religious practices like reading scripture or performing acts in alignment with their faith. For others, it could mean meditating, praying, or practicing yoga.

When we pursue our passions, we're in tune with the divine. What do you truly love to do? Sing, write, paint, create? Your connection to the divine may be religious, spiritual, or simply a profound connection to your truest essence. You'll know you're aligned when you feel a euphoric clarity, when time seems to stand still, when you're open, clear, and powerful. This is alignment. This is why we're here.

REFLECTIVE QUESTIONS & PRACTICES

In the upcoming chapters, we'll talk about connecting with a community, as well as ancestral wisdom. These two aspects are integral to creating your whole self, tapping into your unique power, and clarifying elements of your life. For now, take some time to browse through the questions and exercises below, which will help you fully integrate your body, heart, skills, and connection with the divine into your new path.

Connecting with Your Body:

1. What sensations am I noticing right now, and what might they be telling me?
2. How can I move my body today in a way that feels nurturing and nourishing?
3. What activities made me feel the most free as a child? What did I engage in that helped me lose track of time? How can I bring some of that back into my current life?
4. When was the last time I felt truly present in my body without thinking about the past or future? How did it feel? What was I doing?
5. If I could move my body in a way that felt playful and effortless, what would that look like? How can I invite that into my week or weekend?
6. What sensory experiences—like feeling grass on my toes, sun on my skin, or dancing to a fun song—help me to enjoy the moment?

7. As a child I used to love to _____. What's stopping me from trying it again, and how might it bring joy and connection into my life?

Connecting with Your Heart:

1. What simple daily rituals—like slowly sipping tea without multitasking or taking a deep breath—help me feel nurtured and present? How can I make space for these?

2. When was the last time I truly allowed myself to receive love, support, help, or a compliment? How can I practice opening up my heart to be willing to receive today?

3. What does it feel like to give myself permission to slow down and simply *be* without the pressure to do or achieve? How can I practice that more often?

4. In what ways do I give love to others effortlessly, and how can I start to mirror that tenderness back to myself?

5. How does my heart respond when I create stillness and allow myself to experience the present moment? What helps me linger in that place longer before rushing off to the next task?

Connecting with the World:

1. How do I feel when I spend time in nature? How can I carve out a few moments for this regularly?

2. What aspects of nature do I have access to that I can fit into my schedule for a few moments on the busy days? Putting my feet on grass? Touching a tree? Breathing in fresh air? Letting the sun shine on my face?

3. What elements of nature inspire or calm me the most? What about them do I love?

4. How can I engage my senses more fully when I'm outside?

5. In what ways does nature help settle my nervous system and calm me down during the busiest of days? How long does it take for it to have this effect?

6. What promise can I make to myself about spending more time in nature? Include some promises for big nature immersions for when you have more time, as well as small moments when life is busy.

Connecting with a New Skill:

1. What's one skill I've always wanted to learn? What's currently holding me back?

2. How can I create an opportunity for myself to explore this new skill?

3. What would spending some time each week with this new skill feel like? How would it change how I show up for those around me?

4. How does learning something new create more connection for myself?

5. What mindset shifts can I make to embrace growth and imperfections as I learn a new skill?

6. How might this inspire others around me to do the same?

Connecting with Divine:

1. What does connection with the divine mean to me personally? How do I currently or want to experience that?

2. What moments in my life have made me feel more connected to something greater than myself? How can I invite more of that into my daily life?

3. When do I feel most connected to something greater, whether it be source, god, quantum, the universe, etc.?

4. What practices or rituals, such as prayer, meditation, journaling, gratitude practice, make me feel most aligned with the divine, and how can I make time for them today?

5. How can I trust and surrender more fully to the flow of life?

6. In what ways have I experienced divine guidance through intuition, synchronicities, coincidences, gut feelings, or a sense of inner knowing, and how can I tune in and trust these messages more deeply?

7. What would it feel like to fully surrender and trust that I am supported by an invisible force? How can I practice letting go of control and embracing flow?

CHAPTER 9

Creating Community

Despite living in an age where technology allows us to be in touch with people all over the world, we feel more disconnected than ever, more out of touch than we have in decades. In all actuality, we are more isolated now than we were in the pre-Internet days, and it is taking a toll on our mental health and emotional well-being. A cursory Google search and glance online quickly establishes how worried we are about our children; from never going outside to not having in-person conversations, to losing huge chunks of their time to mindless scrolling, parents are increasingly concerned about how to teach their children to manage online life versus reality.

I'm sure you think about this as much as I do. But have you asked yourself if you're doing the same thing? Are you living an online life more than you're living one based in reality? What are you modeling for your children? Before I became aware of how much of my time was spent staring at a screen, I didn't realize how much of my life I was giving away to being on devices rather than meeting up with my friends. In the past, I've experienced moments of unease while engaging with someone else in real life because I'd literally forgotten how to have in-person conversations. Body language, mirroring, eye contact, modulated vocal response—all of the tiny nuances that go into having a conversation with a real human being are completely null and void when we're online. And where are we most of the time? I'll let that go unanswered.

Once you have discovered your whole self, you will find that she has been yearning not just for connection with you, but with other people as well. She wants to laugh and cry, not in response to an online video where the person on the other end can't see her and respond in kind, but with another person who is directly in front of her. The beautiful thing is that once you get wholly and fully reconnected with your true self, your village will find you. Looking back at the loneliness I felt for so long, even though I was surrounded by people, I realize now that I was lonely for ME. I missed the girl I used to be. The girl who felt free, who laughed, who played, the girl whose life wasn't dictated by her to-do list and what she accomplished, or who she was needed by or what she "should" do. The girl who moved through life in the present moment. Where was that version of me? Using the tools in the Connection Code, I found her. In small moments throughout my days as a middle-aged woman, I got reunited with her again. Through microdosing moments of play, of nurturing, of asking what it was that I needed in this moment, rather than constantly asking myself what everyone else needed, I found her again. And in doing so, my community/village found me. There is a palpable and magnetic energy that exudes from a woman who gets back to herself again. It's attractive, it's contagious, and other women want it. Your people will find you. This is how we actually get that village we constantly hear about. The village of women that truly sees us and loves us for who we are. The real, raw, sometimes messy, sometimes chaotic, sometimes elated, always beautiful TRUE version of us. Boundaries and all.

An APA study released in 2023 found that one in three Americans regularly feels lonely.[10] Additionally, when Americans feel lonely, the number one way they address the situation is to distract themselves by watching TV, listening to podcasts, or scrolling through social media. Rather than changing our situation, we busy ourselves with something else so that we don't have to focus on the feeling.

This is no surprise, of course. As we've talked about before, social media provides instant gratification. Do you want to laugh? How about a good cry? Want to watch another person have a breakdown? What about a feel-good story about an animal rescue center? Try out this video of someone saying no to a public marriage proposal—that will definitely distract you. Good or bad, social media provides a quick fix hit of dopamine when real life feels hard or just uncomfortable. It's a completely passive, no-work solution that can eat up hours of your evening so that you don't have to sit around thinking about how lonely you are.

But guess what? It also keeps you that way.

THE LONELINESS EPIDEMIC

How did we get here? The reasons behind the loneliness experienced by so many people are complex but relatable.

- **Digital Overload**—While social media might keep us updated on all that is going on in the world and other people's lives, it fosters surface-level interactions, leaving us longing for more. Sure, you might feel like that influencer understands you like a sister, but if you passed her on the street, would she know your face? Of course not. It's a one-way relationship where you passively absorb what she says, does, and feels, without any reciprocation. She has no idea what you are saying, doing, or feeling.

- **Life Stages**—Women from their 30s through their 70s are experiencing a variety of life transitions. From finding a partner, to getting married, to starting a family, starting or changing a career, retiring, empty nesting, and becoming a grandparent, women's lives are often dictated by the needs of others, no matter what their age. This can create a life that may seem busy and full, but actually leaves very little room for connecting with others. Is it easier to watch some reels than call a friend? Yes. Is it as rewarding? No.

- **Decline in Friendship Culture**—The 2021 American Time Use Survey found that women are spending less time than ever before on their friendships.[11] For women aged 30 to 70, making new friendships feels even more daunting, especially when our long-standing connections shift and change due to career moves, changes in values, or simply drifting apart.

In order to understand why we're living lonely lives bereft of an actual community, we first need to take a closer look at the modern relationships we invest in and how they are interfering with deeper, more intense connections.

PARASOCIAL RELATIONSHIPS

That influencer who feels like she could be your sister? She's totally not. She doesn't know who you are. But you definitely know everything about her! From her favorite snack to where she went on vacation to her morning skin care routine to that nasty breakup from a month ago, you are in the weeds on the details of her life. Ironically, you might even engage in conversations with other people online who *also* feel like she's their best buddy. You talk about your favorite moments in your non-friend's life, wonder if she's going to land that job interview, and mutually worry when her dog eats a tennis ball. You behave as if this is a real person in your life, worrying about her when you wake up and checking in before you go to sleep.

She's not doing the same for you. Because it's not a real relationship.

A parasocial relationship is one-sided. You may feel emotionally invested, or as if you have a close tie with this person, but there is no reciprocity. She's not thinking about you, she definitely doesn't know that your kid has a head cold, and she isn't going to answer your DM about the fight you had with your husband. Yet . . . how many hours did you "spend" with her this week? How much one-sided conversation was had, as you absorbed everything she said, yet weren't able to respond? What if you'd taken that time to meet up with a real-life friend in a coffee shop or give them a call? These connections with influencers and public figures, although comforting, lack depth and the mutual exchange of a real relationship.

A 2021 study from the Bureau of Labor Statistics found that, on average, Americans spend less than an hour a day socializing—even with people in their own household.[12]

However, they spend triple that amount of time in their parasocial relationships through various forms of media. These one-sided relationships aren't just eating up our time; they're creating a fake feeling of belonging that distracts us from connecting with real people, in real life, in real time.

ASYNCHRONOUS RELATIONSHIPS

An asynchronous relationship is one where the interactions aren't happening in real time. In other words, each person involved isn't experiencing the same knowledge, emotions, or reactions in the same moment. For example, if your friend texts you that she was in a car accident, you have an immediate reaction—your stomach bottoms out, your heart rate picks up, you are immediately flooded with feelings of empathy and concern. But when you finally get a chance to call her back, the situation is settled. The tow truck already came, she was checked out by medics and is back at home with just a little whiplash, and her emotions are under control. She's already processed and reflected on the event, whereas it's still totally new to you—you are experiencing the conversation in very different ways.

It's an extreme example, but you get the idea. Another way to think of an asynchronous interaction is texting. Ever send a text when you were really mad at someone? Did the heat of the moment make you fire off a string of thoughts and feelings that you didn't really reflect on? When they read the text two hours later, they were experiencing your anger at them in *that* moment, and they had all the reactions they would have had if they were right in front of you—shame, guilt, doubt, fear, their own anger. But by the time they respond, you've dealt with your emotions, feel differently, and probably regret sending the text. You can apologize and try to make amends, but now *they're* all riled up and don't have anywhere to put their emotions, because you're already past it.

The delay creates an asynchronous relationship—both parties aren't experiencing the moment at the same time. The same is true if you send a voice note, comment on social media, e-mail, DM, or video message. It lacks the immediacy and spontaneity of in-person connection and conversation. The time delay is a buffer; it doesn't require us to show up authentically, fully, and vulnerably in the moment.

This matters because it impacts our ability to respond to each other. When you are in a disagreement with someone who is right in front of you, you are able to watch their body language and micro-communications, hear the tone of their words, and see the impact of your own. Every aspect of connection is present, in the moment, face-to-face. It's a true, honest, vulnerable, scary place to be—but absolutely necessary to relationships that are deep and fulfilling.

Of course, there are plenty of healthy relationships that have an asynchronous element to them. Do I text my husband throughout the day, and does he read the text hours later? Yes, absolutely. But we'll also be having dinner together in the evening and connecting in a deeper way at that time. This applies in our friendships, as well. You know those giggling fits you can't stop, the ones that spark your friend to start laughing, too? Pretty soon your abs hurt, and you have coffee running out of your nose. You're both still laughing, but you honestly couldn't say why, what was so funny, or even be able to explain it to someone else later. Ever had that experience over text? No, you haven't.

WHY THESE RELATIONSHIPS AREN'T ENOUGH

These two types of relationships constitute the majority of the connections that today's women participate in. They give the illusion of connection but in most cases are surface level at best. More importantly, they fill the space where true connection and community could find us if we allowed it. A parasocial relationship lacks depth, while an asynchronous relationship lacks the energy and richness of real-life face-to-face. In both of these, intimacy is lost. We are never fully seen, fully interacting, fully belonging. So if these relationships are subpar, why do we keep seeking them out and even depend on them?

- **Busyness**—In the days of over-packed schedules filled with work, personal needs, and family responsibilities, there just isn't time to seek out and create deep, meaningful connections. Asynchronous relationships feel less burdensome because they don't require immediate responses or the time and planning required for a physical meetup. These connections can occur on their own terms—eliminating the stress of scheduling conflicts, pressure to reciprocate, or guilt for not being able to show up.

- **Fear**—Opening yourself up to others is risky. We run the risk of being judged. Maybe we're too much, not enough, misunderstood, or worse—rejected. But parasocial and asynchronous connections often feel safer because they are largely one-sided, fostering a feeling of connection without the threat of getting hurt.

- **Masks & Filters**—Our society encourages us to wear masks of perfection, always happy and energetic. Keeping our connections surface level helps prevent anyone from seeing what's truly going on underneath—the silent struggle we all carry. The irony is that the underneath place is where we actually form real connections.

- **Emotional Drain**—After giving so much of ourselves to work, family, and everyone and everything outside of us, many women find it hard to engage in relationships that require more emotional output and energy.

These reasons have kept many women in a cycle of loneliness or surface-level low-pressure interactions and connections. However, recognizing these patterns is the first step toward change. The next step? Taking small, brave actions to break this cycle and step into the richness of real, meaningful connections.

IT'S NOT EITHER/OR—IT'S BOTH/AND

I'm sure you're reading all of this and thinking, *Hey, lady, I text with my group of girls every day and it feels great. I'm not giving it up!* You definitely shouldn't! Listen, I love an audio text as much as the next girl. I use these voice texts to stay connected with friends that live states or even countries away from me. I also love social media; I know it has its drawbacks, and boundaries are crucial, but as someone who has family all over the country, I appreciate the ability to see what's going on in my friends' and families' lives. But I'm aware that I'm only seeing their highlight reel. I'm not really, fully experiencing a deep, fulfilling relationship by liking their Facebook posts.

Likewise, my audio notes are just a placeholder for in-person meetups—which are crucial both to my mental health and the health of the friendship itself. I now make it a point to have a once-a-week meetup with someone in real life, whether it's meeting a girlfriend for coffee or a half-hour chat at school drop-off. When I realize I haven't had a synchronous conversation (where we're both talking to each other and responding in real time) with someone who I typically leave audio notes for, I actually get on the phone or a Zoom with them.

Parasocial and asynchronous relationships aren't by definition unhealthy or even a bad thing to have in your life. It's when they start to take the place of true, authentic connection or are substituted for real-time shared experiences that we begin to feel that pit of loneliness open up inside of us. So . . . how do we fix this?

1. *Get clear on your values and needs.* You're going to put work into finding or creating a community, so let's make sure it's the right one, aligned with who you are or who you want to be. Are you looking for shared interests? Accountability? Support? Inspiration? Do you want friends who are going to get mad at you for not staying up all night drinking with them? Or do you want friends who are going to help you get to spin class on Saturday morning? Who do you want to be? Get clear with yourself so that you can create a community in which that version of you belongs.

2. *Take the initiative.* This can be scary, but you are courageous. Take baby steps and perhaps even start

with low-hanging fruit for practice. Rather than waiting for others to reach out, ask someone to meet for coffee, go for a walk, or go with you to a casual gathering. Begin with people you trust and go from there.

3. *Create opportunities for connection.* Host a potluck, a book club, or an event that is something easy and fun for busy women. I recently hosted a make-and-take workshop with some friends where we made a natural skin care product. We chatted, connected, made an incredible product, and everyone left with something fun that they could use every day.

4. *Identify and focus on shared experiences.* Do things together—fun things that are off the radar of our usual boring days. Go to a dance or unique exercise class, a crafting class like jewelry making or painting with a twist, or try that pole dancing class that looks amazing but you're way too scared to walk into by yourself.

5. *Celebrate milestones.* One thing we don't do enough is celebrate. Acknowledge your friends' birthdays, accomplishments, and life changes within your community to foster a sense of belonging.

6. *Cultivate vulnerability and trust.* Being open and honest yourself encourages other women. Practice in small, safe spaces if needed—in your home with your family, in your mirror with yourself, in your journal, with your bestie, with your mom, your sister, etc. Sharing your own challenges and stories creates a safe space for others to do the same.

7. *Be a good listener.* Showing genuine interest in others' lives creates rapport and connection. If

someone asks you how your day was, don't just unload on them and consider the conversation over. Reciprocate. How was their day? You won't know unless you ask.

8. *Be consistent.* Whether it's hosting a book club the first weekend of the month or meeting up for coffee and yoga on Saturday mornings, consistent meetups build momentum and cadence, and strengthen bonds.

FIND OR CREATE YOUR OWN LOCAL COMMUNITY

Once you get to know yourself again, once you get back to remembering what it is that lights you up, that fills your cup, that helps you incorporate play and joy again, you may just find yourself feeling pulled to some new and fun activities. It's amazing what you can find when you start looking for it, whether it be a local class at your community center on a hobby you have always wanted to try but were afraid you were too old, or all of a sudden you might see a sign at your local coffee shop (that you somehow never noticed) for a meetup of women looking to do Zumba or a local book club together.

There is a part of our brain that will literally show us what we're ready to see and will block us when we aren't. It's called the reticular activating system (RAS) and is often nicknamed the "gatekeeper" as it filters out sensory information. It limits our ability to view any perceived "irrelevant" information. What does this mean? It means that if for so long you never paid attention to anything for you, opportunities to play, connect, etc., you would have never seen them. And now, as it becomes more of your focus and the subject of questions you're asking yourself (amid the 30,000 subconscious decisions and questions we ask ourselves every day), you will actually start to see it. The week I decided I wanted to take an adult gymnastics class, I found one at our children's gymnasium. I could have "seen" a flyer multiple times for that, but because it wasn't my focus YET, my brain didn't consciously register it. If you don't believe that this exists or how powerful the RAS is in our lives, think about the last time you were car shopping. Or even before you ACTUALLY went car shopping and you had some idea of what color of car or what kind of car you desired. All of a sudden, you started to see these cars EVERYWHERE on the road. There wasn't all of a sudden more of them; your RAS just got the signal that these were important and so stopped filtering them out. Aligning your focus to get clear on what you desire is a VERY powerful way to attract or to actually SEE all the opportunities right in front of you.

REFLECTIVE QUESTIONS & EXERCISES

True connection starts with knowing yourself, and a community begins with cultivating the relationships that you already have. The questions below will help you find your people!

1. Who inspires and/or elevates me?
2. Where can I find people who share my values? What are my values?
3. How can I nurture the aligned friendships that I currently have and value?

4. What is something I've always wanted to do but haven't felt I had the time? What have I felt too selfish to make time for in the past?

5. Where can I find fun "experts" to help walk my community through a shared experience? Examples: dance instructors, tarot card readers, cooking classes, yoga, etc.

CHAPTER 10

Coming Home: Ancestral Wisdom & Alignment

In the quiet firelit circles and communities of our ancestors, women moved through life in sync with the natural rhythms around them. They were guided by and honored the cycles of the moon, the turning of the seasons, and the innate wisdom of their own bodies. Their focus was externally attuned in ways that we've spoken about—constantly monitoring for threats and danger, while also being on the lookout for edible plants while they went about one of their main duties of foraging. At the same time, they were tapped into their inner wisdom, clarity, and wholeness in a way that women today struggle to find time to connect to.

In earlier chapters we've discussed how our ego operates in a focused status, constantly monitoring our surroundings and making assessments about how our actions and speech are being accepted, or rejected, by others. As women, we're also highly attuned to the people around us, as our role as caretakers has taught us to be. Our ability to be productive by juggling all our external responsibilities is amazing, but it comes at the expense of our well-being, because we're never accessing or nurturing our own internal life. This way of disconnected living has us feeling depleted and unfulfilled. We're merely spending our days checking off boxes and not truly experiencing or enjoying our lives.

Our ancestors lived in a state of harmony, meeting the needs of their families and communities while also honoring their own needs, rhythm, intuition, and connection with self. Their self-care was just vastly different from what we have been sold—sometimes quite literally. In a world where we've been taught to seek out whatever we want and need to feel happy *outside* of us, our self-care tools are mostly external: massages, pedicures, manicures, weekend retreats, girls' nights, and facials, to name a few.

Our ancestors had access to tools that connected and aligned them at any moment in time. There was no guilt for leaving their babies with another woman for too long while they went out for a spa day, no need to seek out the nearest salon for a cute new cut and blowout so she could feel her best. These women understood that self-connection wasn't selfish, that it wasn't something outside of them that they needed to chase after, and that it was a necessary piece of being a whole human. They moved through life with a quiet assuredness guided by external responsibilities, while their internal guide never lost sight of who they were and how they could stay aligned with themselves. This awareness allowed them to live in true alignment and wholeness, experiencing a sense of fulfillment and belonging that many of us need and crave today.

We can create our own inner balance and connection again. We can peel back the outer layers and tune in to our inner thoughts for guidance and companionship while still showing up for the people and responsibilities in our lives. We can bridge the gap between our external and internal worlds. It's a win-win scenario.

This begins when we start to recognize that taking time for ourselves is not a luxury but a necessity, and we do that by leaning in and learning more about ourselves not just as individuals, but also as a group. What do women in general need? What power and skills did our female ancestors have that allowed for their lifestyle? One of the greatest tools for truly accessing the wealth of information that exists inside our own bodies is through understanding our cycles.

I'm sure that when I say cycles, you automatically think of your menstrual cycle and the hormones in your body. And yes, those do play a critical role in your well-being; however, there's another cycle at work within your body every day that very few people know about—the cycle of your brain waves. Aligning and working with your brain waves is a tool that can help you on any day, and the knowledge of how to implement this in your daily life will open up a whole new world for you.

DAILY RHYTHM: ALIGNING WITH YOUR BRAIN WAVES

Beyond our monthly cycles, our brains also follow a natural rhythm throughout the day. Just as the women who came before us tapped into the moon to help monitor their monthly flow, we can tap into the daily fluctuations of our brain waves to create ease, focus, insight, clarity, creative output, and rest. Rather than forcing the brain to perform at peak productivity at all times, we can sync into our optimal states throughout the day, recognize the power and importance of each type of brain wave, and realize that we don't have to be going a hundred miles an hour, twenty-four hours a day, seven days a week.

In fact, we're not meant to.

Brain states—those natural rhythms of the mind that influence everything from creativity and focus to relaxation and intuition—are like different gears in a car. Each one is designed for a specific purpose, helping you navigate life with more ease and flow. The best part? You already have access to these powerful states; you just need to know how to tap into them. Yogis and Buddhist monks have long used them to achieve deep states of meditation, inner peace, and heightened awareness. But you don't have to spend a lifetime studying in order to achieve this. You can boost your creativity, find clarity, and feel more aligned in your daily life just by learning about the natural processes going on inside your own mind and how to harness the distinct and powerful forces of each of them.

Once you learn how, you'll be able to shift from stress, overwhelm, or feeling scattered to calm, clarity, and creativity in less than five minutes. And, unlike therapy, supplements, or even a gym session, these tools are already within you. You can access them anytime, anywhere—whether it's in the middle of the morning chaos, after a tense meeting at work, or during a challenging moment with your kids. How incredible would it feel to know that *you* brought yourself back to center—not by relying on something external, but by igniting your own power from within?

Your brain operates at different frequencies throughout the day, depending on your activity and mental state. These brain wave states influence everything—your focus, your creativity, your stress levels, and even how connected you feel to yourself and others. Our brain waves are like individual people, each with their own unique personality. And like people, they each have their own aspects, qualities, and circumstances in which they shine.

Theta—the Dreamer

Theta is a dreamy artist. Her mantra is: When the world feels slow, theta runs the show. She is a whimsical, free-spirited person who loves daydreaming, exploring ideas, and diving deep into her imagination. She's the one who helps you tap into your intuition, uncover hidden insights, and heal emotional wounds through creativity and reflection. She is intuitive, emotional, and a little mysterious. She thrives in quiet, reflective moments and loves vision boards.

Theta waves are at their height when you first wake up. Theta waves exist primarily in that space between the dream world and the real world. By lingering in this space, we get access to intuition, wisdom, and creativity. It's here that we can transmit creative solutions to our problems. Waking up is the perfect time for introspection, asking questions, and sitting with ourselves. It's a time for expansive thinking where we can get beyond the *what if* or *I can't/because* thoughts holding us back. This is where we can access more limitless thinking and problem-solving. This is the gateway between our subconscious and conscious mind, and there are lots of incredible treasures that exist in this space.

Theta is broken when we are exposed to white or blue light, either from lamps or—you guessed it—our phones. Do you wake up and reach for your phone first thing in the morning? I used to. I thought this was how I got caught up and reconnected—the perfect way to start the day, right? It turns out that all I was doing was interrupting my theta waves, invading the space that the dreamer needed in order to transfer powerful thoughts and ideas from my subconscious mind into my conscious mind. When I was making the transition to honoring my theta waves, I had some anxiety related to not being able to fit everything in if I wasn't getting to it first thing in the morning. But I soon realized that my early morning brain waves were just as important as my "on the clock" waves that would kick in later in the day.

The great news is that the theta state can be tapped into and even extended by making use of a five-minute morning plan. A great start to introducing this concept into your life is to create a sit spot for yourself. This is a spot that you can go to right from your bed, because if you stay in your bed for your theta time, you likely might just drift back to sleep. The goal is to be awake, but sleepy, so set up a spot that's cozy, but not too cozy. I have a PEMF grounding mat, a pillow I lean on, and an amber book light. Similar to how a person wanting to hit the 6 A.M. gym class ensures success by laying out their clothes the night before, having a space prepared ahead of time means that you don't have to move through an entire process of decision making—What pillow do I want? Where is my fuzzy blanket?—in order to enjoy your early morning me-time.

When you wake you simply make your way to your sit spot. Get quiet and give your thoughts a space. Know that at first it will probably feel like you are doing it wrong, but please know as long as you get yourself here and don't pull yourself out of theta by going online, you're doing it right! When all your to-dos of the day come up, see if you can let them drift away and just create space. Maybe there is anger coming up, or overwhelm, or a sense of hyper-speed about the tasks required of you that day. Theta is where you have access to thinking outside the box, so it's a great time to get clarity. Ask yourself questions, and remember this space is where intuition and inner wisdom shine.

Once you begin fully experiencing theta, you will recognize when your brain is in theta throughout the day—it doesn't just happen in the morning! We also get into theta when we are doing something that doesn't require a lot of thinking, and we can zone out and daydream a bit. Ever had a great idea come to you in the shower? You've got theta to thank for that. Imagine what theta can share with you when you create space for her during her time of the day to shine.

Speaking of shining, this is a great place to introduce the idea of different spectrums of light and the impact they can have on your brain waves. Simply put, our bodies are still operating from ancient DNA, and our brains weren't made to be active during non-daylight hours. The only light source in our ancestors' lives after the sun went down was shades of amber and red from firelight.

But our modern world can re-create daylight at any time—at dusk or even in the dead of night. If you're burning the midnight oil, literally, the white and blue light created from your screens and electric lighting convinces your brain that it's daytime and interrupts your circadian rhythm. The end result is that your brain doesn't get the healing, regenerating time that it needs in order to function well, because it always believes that it's go-time.

But you don't want to go to bed at 6:30 in the winter, do you? Neither do I! Luckily, there are ways around this. In our home, if the sun is not up yet, the only light in our house is red.

This happened in our home gradually over time, and it feels so good that I don't even need to remember to switch the lights anymore. My brain and body (as well as our kids) crave it. And it doesn't need to be overwhelming or expensive. I grabbed some red light bulbs on Amazon (under $10) and slowly added one into a lamp in each of our main rooms. When the sun goes down, all overhead lighting in our home goes off, and the lamps go on. It feels so good in fact that I even put a red light filter onto our fridge light so when I go to grab some yummy organic heavy cream in the morning for my coffee, I'm welcomed with warm, nurturing, alpha and theta supportive lighting rather than being blasted into beta and fast tracking away from nurturing vibes and right into my to-do list for the day. If we blast our brains with bright lighting too early in the morning or too late at night, the brain doesn't get the healing and regenerative time it needs to function in its optimal state, because it always believes it is go-time. Light coming through our eyes has a direct influence on when our bodies go into go-mode and when they go into restore-and-regenerate mode. Restore-and-regenerate mode allows things like the lymph system of our brains, melatonin production, growth hormone secretion, cellular repair and DNA restoration, immune system regulation, cortisol suppression and stress recovery, tissue growth and muscle recovery, as well as blood pressure and cardiovascular regulation. The constant presence of blue and white light from our home lights and our screens means that all of these crucial processes are limited, as our brains believe it's not the right time for those healing theta and delta waves.

So grab yourself some red light. There are some great therapeutic options, as well as simple red light bulbs you can place in lamps for use when there is no sunlight. This doesn't need to cost a fortune, but if you match the light in your home and work environment as closely as possible to the light outside and rely on red light only once it's dark outside, your body, mind, and soul will thank you.

Alpha—the Connector

Alpha is a calm, grounded yoga instructor who encourages you to breathe, relax, and stay present in the moment. Her mantra is: For a mind that's clear, draw alpha near. She's all about finding balance, whether it's through journaling, meditation, or simply pausing to appreciate life. She loves morning rituals and afternoon resets. She teaches us that slowing down isn't unproductive—it's the key to staying connected and creative. Alpha is the transition from Theta as we're continuing to wake up, but *before* we get into logistics and to-dos for the day. Where theta is a space for deep intuition—meditation, affirmations, and subconscious exploration—alpha is a space for journaling, mindfulness, and light movement.

This is also where we achieve what is called a flow: a mental state of complete immersion and focus in an activity, where time seems to disappear, actions feel effortless, and creativity and performance peak. Flow state is that feeling when you're fully immersed in something you love—whether it's a physical activity that gets you out of your busy head and into your body, fully immersing yourself in a great book, or effortlessly balancing work and family life with a sense of calm focus and ease. These moments happen on their own, but we often have no way of knowing how to intentionally create them.

One of the best ways to slip into alpha and get all the benefits of this brain state is to team up with her when it's her peak time in the early morning. If for whatever reason you missed out or want to create more pockets later in the day, there are some great ways to access alpha waves at any time.

- *Sensory Engagement:* A great question I ask myself to help get me into the present moment is: *What do I see, hear, and smell?* Activating our senses is a fast track to alpha.

- *Go Outside:* Being in nature is a great way to kickstart alpha waves. The popular online saying "you need to touch grass" isn't only a meme—it's the truth!

- *Creative Expression*: Remember the moment those adult coloring books had? Those are great, and I highly recommend tools like that as they get us into alpha. A puzzle is also great for kickstarting alpha. If you have a table that can be cleared and used just for an ongoing puzzle project, it's not only a great way to find your alpha, but also invites others in the household to participate as well.

- *Playfulness and Curiosity:* Engaging in lighthearted play is a wonderful way to activate alpha. I love a good five-minute ride around my neighborhood on my bike. My friend dribbles a basketball and shoots hoops in front of his house. Another friend bought herself a pair of tap shoes and puts them on between Zoom meetings, tapping out the time in between her next duties.

- *Flickering Flames:* Ever notice that feeling you get when you stare at a fire, and it's like you're in a zone? That's alpha. When we stare at a flickering flame, mirror neurons in our brain are activated. Our mirror neurons are brain cells that help us understand and copy what we see in our environment. When we see someone smile, look sad, or cross their arms over their chest, we subconsciously mirror these feelings or actions, helping us connect to one another. When we look at a flame, and these brain cells are activated, they match the frequency of the flame, which happens to be the same frequency of alpha, instantly shifting us into a calm and connected state.

If you've ever experienced moments throughout the day where you just feel balanced, you're feeling your alpha waves. Often when we find ourselves in this place—after a workout or coffee with friends—the next move is to hop on our phones to check what we missed. Instead of lingering in this place of contentment, we tend to immediately see who needs us, what we need to do next, or check in with someone else . . . not ourselves. If you can just give yourself a few moments to sit in that space and soak it all in, you will reap the benefits of alpha, improving mental clarity and emotional balance, and setting a more balanced tone for the rest of your day. Make it a goal after your next workout, dog-walking stint, or face-to-face meetup with friends to not pick up your phone for at least five minutes.

Beta—the Achiever

Beta is a dedicated sprinter and go-getter who thrives on speed, focus, and getting things done. She prides herself on checking things off her to-do list and feels energized by progress. She is productive, energetic, driven—but prone to exhaustion if she doesn't slow down. She reminds us that pushing forward is great, but balance and rest are essential to stay in the race. Just like any runner, she needs to pace herself and take water breaks, or she'll burn out. Her mantra is: If I rest, I rust. Because beta is in a constant state of productivity, it's our job to keep tabs on her and let her know when it's time to take a break.

Beta is our prime work force wave, and it serves a great purpose . . . but it is also the space that our society honors the most, which means that we try to stay here, constantly urging our brains to do more, give more, be more. And much like a physical body that never stops running, it will eventually break down. When we overwork beta by keeping her going all through the day and into the late hours of the night, we burn her out. That feeling of absolute exhaustion, of not having any gas left in the tank or nothing left to give, is a great indicator that you've pushed Beta to her limits.

If you have spent a lot of time in beta and need to give her a break, you can easily do so by engaging in any of the activities that get you back into alpha. You'll know when you have successfully slipped from beta back into alpha. It will feel like taking a deep breath after a long day. You will be focused on the moment in front of you, rather than ruminating over the future or the past. You'll be able to be completely present with the people around you, whether it be your loved ones or the checkout clerk at the store. You'll stop multitasking and get a more linear focus. You'll feel lighter, your shoulders will drop, your breathing will regulate, and you'll feel a sense of joy, ease, and calm wash over you. You'll feel connected again. When you give beta this little break, she comes back online energized and ready to perform, not run-down and ragged, catapulting through the next hoop.

Gamma—the Visionary

Gamma is the goal. She is the reward for doing it "right." She is your brain's electric sparkle and high-wave-frequency flow state that magically manifests after you have made space for theta and alpha. She brings the breakthrough, the download, the ah-ha moment, and the idea that lands so beautifully it feels like it came from someone else. It's you—you are that powerful and clairvoyant when in alignment. But she won't respond to force; she only responds to flow.

Here's the important takeaway. In those moments where your ego might attempt to nudge you that you are being unproductive by taking a few moments to daydream (theta), do a puzzle, play, light a candle (alpha), your whole self/

true self voice can remind/quiet her that these moments are priming your brain for gamma. Theta makes you receptive, and alpha makes you present, allowing gamma to magically arrive with insight and ease. Her presence is proof that you're living with your brain, not against it. Her mantra is: Flow opens the portal; I bring the spark.

Delta—the Healer

Delta is a nurturing, wise grandmother who insists on rest, deep sleep, and taking care of yourself. She knows that healing happens when we slow down completely and embrace stillness, and she helps us create space in an evening ritual to do so. She's all about early bedtimes, deep breaths, and nighttime rituals. No white light, no finishing off e-mails, or overuse of screens. Her focus is getting you into a state so you can get the deep sleep that is required for healing to occur. She reminds us that true restoration happens when we surrender to rest and trust the process. Her mantra is: When it's time to heal, delta takes the wheel.

Luckily, delta isn't only available to us when we sleep, and we can learn how to transition into that liminal state of delta with some easy tips and tools for evening time.

- Limit or avoid blue and white light from indoor lighting and screens. Much like theta, delta is interrupted by the brain believing it's daylight. Making use of red lighting in your home will help you slip more easily into your delta waves when it's time.

- Consciously shift out of work mode into transition to sleep mode. This isn't the time to wrap up e-mails and work on challenges left over from the day. Remind yourself you'll be more effective at that during beta time tomorrow—especially if you

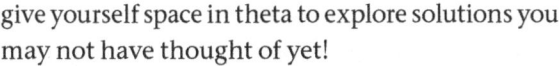

give yourself space in theta to explore solutions you may not have thought of yet!

- Lower the temperature where you will be sleeping. A cooler environment triggers melatonin and signals to the body that sleep time is near. It also activates our parasympathetics—the "rest and digest" aspect of our nervous system—which helps the brain slow down and enter delta.

THE DAILY BRAIN

Each day, we have the opportunity to work with the rhythm of our brain or against it. Working with it, and knowing how to identify which state you are in, will help bring balance to your daily life.

Many of us spend much too much time in beta. We are asking our runner to run from the moment we wake until the moment we sleep. We don't give our brains a break until they hit a brick wall, at which point we mindlessly scroll through Netflix or our phones (puts us into beta brain wave) because we're tanked. Think of alpha as beta's quick sip of water for that overtaxed runner. It doesn't take long but yields massive results. These small dips into and out of the various flow states are what allow us to stay connected to our internal guidance system, no matter what is going on around us. Our brains and bodies are not intended to live in hyper-speed and overdrive at all times; we need moments of rest and recovery. Allowing ourselves time in alpha, theta, gamma, and delta is what creates that pause and space.

For a busy career woman, overtaxing beta might look like attending back-to-back meetings and checking e-mails in the morning and late into the evening in an effort to catch up, only to find that she is fried when it actually comes time to prepare for that big presentation. A mama living in beta is often juggling schedules, school pickups, dinners, meal planning, and helping with homework. We push through our day in constant beta mode, and when bedtime comes and we get the opportunity to actually connect with our loved ones, or even be present with ourselves, we can't. We're done. Instead of being present, we're irritable or detached, not because we don't care, but because our brain is stuck in beta and doesn't see some snuggling, reading, or winding down as a productive use of our time.

This could look like getting to the end of the day, still feeling ramped up and unable to sit and just BE with a book, wind-down routine, etc., and so we scroll our phones or turn on a show. We do this because we are so wired and don't know how to unwind. We need a bridge, and the bridge is built by leaning into the rhythm of your brainwaves. Choosing a task or activities in these moments that will get us into alpha makes all the difference. Living in alignment and flow with your natural brain waves will connect you more fully not only to yourself, but to your world and those around you. By taking time for yourself and nourishing your mind by enjoying the messages of theta, the insights of alpha, the insights of gamma, and the restoration that delta has to offer, you will achieve a balance that our female ancestors were intuitively aware of and made use of in their daily lives in order to maintain their connections to self and community.

THE 5 P'S OF BRAIN WAVE ALIGNMENT

Pause: *Morning / Theta*—Begin your day by pausing to dream, reflect, and tune in to your subconscious with activities like visualization or meditation.

Prepare: *Mid-Morning / Alpha*—Journal, set intentions, and clear mental clutter to create space for focused work.

Produce: *Late Morning to Afternoon / Beta*—Dive into deep and intense work, problem-solving, and output when your brain is alert and most productive.

Plan: *Late Afternoon / Alpha & Beta*—Handle logistics, e-mails, and to-do lists when your focus naturally starts to shift.

Peace: *Evening / Theta & Delta*—Wind down with relaxation activities and practices that promote rest and recovery, preparing your body and mind for deep sleep.

*Where gamma fits: Gamma is the reward that arrives during or after

- Alpha—when you're in creative flow
- Beta—when you're focused and engaged in aligned action
- Theta—during meditation or grounding moments of listening
- Gamma—the reward that arrives when we live in alignment. The clarity and insight that appears when your nervous system knows it's safe to receive.

Theta	Gamma
The whisper—"I feel I need to rest today"	The lightning—full body YES
Helps you FEEL into what's true	Helps you SEE it clearly
Slow, sacred knowing	Fast, electric, energetic
Opens the door	Turns on the light

You don't need more willpower, and you can stop beating yourself up for feeling unmotivated or burnt out. There's nothing wrong with you, you're just often living out of SYNC. This simple daily flow chart will help you get back into alignment with your natural brain wave patterns so you can move through your day feeling more grounded, intentional, and a whole lot more you.

*Note, the times listed are simply examples of windows of time. Feel free to replace with your own as it fits your life. Aim to spend at LEAST 5 minutes (ideally closer to 15 or 20) in theta and alpha before beta each day. Also, the same goes for the end of the day. Aim for at LEAST 5 minutes in the evening for winding down (ideally about 20 to 30 minutes).

THETA: THE MAGIC OF THETA: ACCESS TO INSIGHTS AND CLARITY

Time	Action Step	Avoid This
5–7 A.M.	Listen	Screentime, white/blue light

ALPHA: THE MAGIC OF ALPHA: FLOW STATE, ENHANCES PEAK PERFORMANCE, HEART OPENING, GETS YOU INTO THE PRESENT MOMENT

Time	Action Step	Avoid This
7–9 A.M.	Journal, daydream, nature, light movements, do a puzzle, color, look at a flickering flame (candle)	News, social media, scrolling

BETA: THE MAGIC OF BETA: ENERGETIC, DRIVEN, "GET IT DONE" MODE

Time	Action Step	Avoid This
9–5 P.M.	Get it done. Whatever your main tasks are for the day. Check off your to-do list.	Distractions, multitasking, interruptions (put phone and e-mails on "do not disturb") *Alpha and theta BREAKS recommended

*During BETA time it is strongly recommended that you take frequent short, intentional breaks that get you into ALPHA or THETA.

Suggestions: Five minutes in nature without your phone, playing, moving your body, dancing, listening to music, getting some sunshine, walking with a friend, daydreaming.

The key is these breaks are screen-free and allow your beta brain the break she deserves. At the end of the day, this translates into getting it all done *while* feeling calm, centered, and aligned. Satisfied instead of scattered.

ALPHA AND THETA EVENING WIND DOWN: THE MAGIC OF THE EVENING WIND DOWN: IT PREPS YOUR BODY FOR RESTORATIVE, REGENERATIVE SLEEP

Time	Action Step	Avoid this
After dinner until about 9 P.M.	Whatever feels nurturing—read a book, take a bath, light a candle. Red and amber light sources are best for this time (circadian rhythm supporting light sources)	Getting those "last minute" things done. Finishing e-mails, work tasks, making major decisions. Avoid white and blue light and screen usage when possible. Although, cuddling up for a movie fits here.

DELTA: THE MAGIC OF DELTA: DEEP HEALING, RESTORATION, NERVOUS SYSTEM RESET

Time	Action Step	Avoid This
By 10 P.M. latest	Sleep	Getting on phone if awake in middle of night

This chart is just the beginning. As you get to know and start aligning more with your natural rhythm instead of pushing against it, you will experience more clarity, joy, and ease through your day. But what if you could take this knowledge even deeper?

You now know that your brain follows a daily rhythm. Your body moves through a monthly cycle too, and you can align your brain waves with this cycle. Learning to align your brain waves with your menstrual cycle, or the lunar cycle if you're no longer bleeding, helps you unlock a powerful layer of connection that you've been missing out on for far too long.

Our brains and hormones don't work in isolation. They are intimately involved with one another. Estrogen, progesterone, and testosterone not only impact our reproductive system, they directly influence our brains. Estrogen enhances dopamine and serotonin—two feel-good neurotransmitters—boosting mood, motivation, and mental clarity.

Progesterone has a calming effect on the nervous system, promoting GABA, that supports relaxation, intuition, and emotional sensitivity. Testosterone offers a short surge in confidence and assertiveness around ovulation, giving us a hardy dose of what I like to call peacock energy. We're feeling magnetic, radiant, and want to be seen, share our voices, and fan our feathers a little.

This hormonal dance, influencing our neurochemistry and shaping our brain wave states, will make us feel more outward and inspired, and give us a burst of momentum or a need/desire to surrender, depending on the phase.

The women who came before us saw these cycles not as inconvenient interruptions, as we often do in our modern-day life, but rather as sacred guides. During menstruation, women would retreat to red tents together, not because they were weak or slow or tired, not because there was something wrong with them, because their desire to do it all was missing; they retreated because they were powerful. They knew this part of their cycle was not a time to power through but to tune in, to go inward and to listen. They honored their bodies' need for rest and saw it as a portal to revelation.

Rather than an inconvenience, they saw their cycle as the *compass*—their internal guidance system telling them when to lead, when to create, when to connect, and when to retreat.

Today, many of us have lost that internal guide and connection. We're fighting against our bodies, shaming and guilting ourselves for not always showing up with peacock energy. We're tired and burnt out and think there's something wrong with us. We've simply lost touch with our alignment, but we can reclaim it simply through rhythm, awareness, and small daily shifts in our choices that honor our bodies. This isn't about perfection—it's partnership with our bodies.

Menses/ Lunar Phase	Embodied Rhythm	Energetic Theme	Hormonal Shifts	Optimal Brain Wave State	Do This/ Action Step
Menstruation/New Moon	Inward	Rest, reflect, shed & return	Estrogen & progesterone low, hormonal reset begins	Theta + Delta	Journal, daydream, visualize, let go, boundaries. Clear space to move forward in alignment
Follicular/ Waxing Moon	Inspired	Creative & Clarity	Estrogen rising/prep for ovulation	Alpha + Gamma	Brainstorm, plan, start new projects
Ovulation/ Full Moon	Outward	Connection & Visibility	Estrogen peaks, slight rise in testosterone	Beta + Gamma	Speaking, collaborating, expansive thinking & living
Luteal/ Waning Moon	*Momentum + Surrender	Focus & Completion	Progesterone rises then drops, estrogen falls	Beta + Alpha	Finish tasks, organize, boundaries

*Momentum to Surrender (luteal phase is a bridge/portal) starts with momentum and ends in surrender. Honoring the duality prevents burnout and fosters an effective shift into the next phase.

Aligning with our brain waves gives us permission to no longer live through the lens of "should" or "supposed to." No need to "push through" anymore when you're exhausted. Understanding these cycles empowers us to no longer think our emotions and feelings and/or energy (or lack thereof) indicates that there is something wrong with us. They are our signals, and when we follow, listen, and align with them, we drop in and come home to a version of us that is more grounded and powerful, simply by creating more space to be our true selves.

REFLECTIVE EXERCISE:

Grab your journal and ask yourself, "How can I honor each phase this month?"

You've now learned how your brain/nervous system flows through its rhythm each day. But it's not enough just to know your rhythm. You need to live it.

And most women don't, not because they don't care, but because they don't know how AND because they've been taught that slowing down, taking time for themselves, is selfish. That stillness is unproductive. That answers and solutions live OUTSIDE of them, on the Internet, in advice from a friend, on social media, or by getting that thing, whether it's the right outfit, job, career, house, relationship, etc.

The Self-WITH Practice/Pathway:

The Self-WITH Practice/Pathway is your way to come home. To create an inward anchor within yourself that you can always access amid the craziest moments of life. In those moments where you're running late, hit traffic, spill your coffee, you are no longer focusing attention outward on your perfect friend who has it all together, or that spa day you need, or the getaway you are craving. Through this practice you can ALWAYS have something to easily turn to in all of life's toughest moments, and it's within you. This is how YOU become your safe place.

And now let's walk through the simple, science-backed practices that you can actually fit into your life in just a few minutes a day. Because the tools we need are not ones that require us to DO more. How refreshing to know that you already have it all within reach, and now you'll know for certain how to access it.

SELF-WITH (noun):

A daily practice of self-connection rooted in nervous system awareness, emotional regulation, and intentional presence.

A state in which you consciously slow down, turn inward, and hold space for your whole self—mentally, emotionally, and physically—rather than seeking external validation or distraction. Through micro-moments of mindfulness, intuitive listening, and compassionate self-inquiry, being self-with offers you a sustainable path to inner alignment and well-being.

Becoming self-with is a new way of relating to your nervous system, intentionally aligning with your body's natural rhythm and truth. Each letter is a gentle reminder and practice. It's a road map home.

S: Slow down before you speed up: Connecting with your body and rhythm first before the day gets busy.

E: Exhale the outside world: Let go of what isn't yours to carry. This is your time to connect with you, your voice, your needs, your desires.

L: Listen to YOU first: The clarity you are craving

> doesn't come from someone else, or social media, or your e-mails, or your to-do list. It comes from your own stillness and your inner truth, and through practice you'll begin to hear it.
>
> **F:** FEEL what's real: No more numbing or distracting ourselves out of our feelings. Your feelings aren't the problem; they're the portal, the road map back to your truth, your alignment, and getting your needs met.
>
> **W:** Wake with intention: Before the world comes in, connect with yourself. Power doesn't have to come from a plan; it comes from presence.
>
> **I:** Inward anchor: The answers aren't out there—they're in here. The self-with practice strengthens your ability to pause, listen, and reconnect with yourself in any moment, especially the ones that feel the most overwhelming. Your focus is no longer on reaching for something outside of yourself or numbing—you have built the tools and trust to turn inward and stay.
>
> **T:** Trust the voice within: Your nervous system knows what you need. It just needs space to be heard. This is where you relearn and remember how to trust yourself again.
>
> **H:** Hold space for your whole self: The bright parts, the shadows, the strong parts, and the sacred ones. All of you belongs.

A Morning Story: Elise

It's 6:15 A.M.

Elise opens her eyes and immediately feels it—the familiar heaviness of the day.

Regret from the day before. A sense of worry about something she said. A pang of guilt and shame for all she didn't get done. The voices are loud before she has even fully woken up and gotten out of bed.

She reaches for her phone just like she does every morning. It's a lifeline and an escape from this feeling. She scrolls most mornings just hoping to feel anything different. Praying the outside world will have an idea, a solution, an opportunity, or at least help her feel differently. Even numbness would feel better than her current state.

But today, she stopped.

She decides to try being self-with.

She sits up, grounds her feet on the floor beneath her.

Half asleep, she saunters to her sit spot, a barely carved-out spot on the corner of her couch with a blanket while the world and her home is still asleep. She gets her book in hand. She connects with her breath. She reads. Even if it's just one page. She feels herself soften. One page turns into another and another. Ten minutes go by and she feels lighter, refreshed, inspired, and motivated. It all doesn't feel so heavy. She has gotten herself into alignment in a matter of moments. She didn't fix anything. She didn't solve the world's problems. She showed up. With herself.

An Evening Story: Maren

It's 9:01 P.M.

The house and world are finally quiet.

Her body is still buzzing from the day, but her heart feels unsettled, hollow.

She had a snack, she scrolled, checked her e-mails, social media, maybe even peeked at what's going on in the world, but none of it fulfilled her. She still feels unsettled, unmoved by it all.

This moment is when she would normally just climb into bed, hoping somehow tomorrow will be magically different.

But instead, she decides to practice in a new way. She isn't aiming for perfection, just ventures to dip her toes in and test the waters.

She grabs her journal and writes two sentences.

"What did I need today?"

"Why didn't I create space for that?"

Those two questions change everything for her. She hears her answers. Maybe she writes it, perhaps she just listens. She gains clarity. She breathes. It's not perfect, but she's present. With this moment, with herself.

She is practicing being self-with, and that changes everything.

The self-with practice does not require perfection, just a willingness. A choice to stop searching outside of yourself for all the answers. A decision to stop ignoring and abandoning your needs and desires. Maybe even a quiet or loud, "I'm done doing it this way." All that is required is micro-moments, a bit of courage, and now, you are equipped with the tools.

Part 3

STAYING ALIGNED

CHAPTER 11

Holding Alignment

Now that you are armed with clarity, awareness, and great tools, let's get real for a moment. Even in the best of circumstances, *life* is going to happen. There will be days when you wake up and ride out your previous story and fall back into old habits. Whether it's because you didn't sleep well, your kids got sick, you didn't have the time or energy to engage in staying aligned, there will be moments and days when you fall off course.

It will be different though. This time when you fall off track, you won't just do it subconsciously and think you're destined to fail, like all of the other supposedly transformative life changes you've tried before. You will realize that you are making a conscious *choice* to do so, and that is the major win. Let me explain.

When it happens *this* time, when your kid does something and you're about to snap at them, or the car in front of you brakes too hard and your hand is hovering over the horn, there will be a split second before you react when you *know what's coming.* There is a moment, often very short, where there is a downbeat, a space where a choice occurs. This **pause** is your power, a place for you to recognize that you're about to backslide—and that's okay! Don't let it be a reason for you to give up on yourself. Don't use this as your proof that nothing you do ever sticks.

Instead, be grateful for falling off course. Be thankful for these very human moments that remind you why nine times out of ten, you chose the new way. There is even a space here for you to thank the experience of failure for showing you what your life *used* to look and feel like. Thank it for reminding you how disempowered you used to feel. Remember how you weren't able to control yourself when these moments of complete overwhelm would occur, and most importantly, you had little idea of how to prevent them, or to regulate yourself after they happened. Wow! How different things are now!

Look at you, taking advantage of those few moments throughout the day to check in, breathe, get in nature, tune in to your body, put your hand on your heart, ask what you need, and be willing to receive. Look at how they're all stacking and adding up. Recognize how vastly different it feels when you don't make every incident or mistake just another indicator that you're destined to fail. These human moments are an opportunity for you to remember what life used to be like and how far you've come, even if it's still new. These moments of losing yourself will likely get fewer and fewer, and you will know in an instant how to get yourself back.

As I've said before, I love the word *practice* because it gives us permission to not do it perfectly every time. Staying in alignment isn't about perfection. It's about progress, consistency, and self-compassion. Each misstep gives us an opportunity to pause, reflect, and realign with our whole selves. Alignment is a practice, not a destination, and there's an easy acronym to help you in those moments when perhaps you slip a bit.

P: PAUSE AND ACKNOWLEDGE

Next time you fall out of alignment—maybe you lose your footing in a big meeting or social encounter and play small and hide your true self—take a breath, notice and recognize the feeling. This pause gives you the choice to course correct, and in the few instances where you choose the old way it will at least be obvious to you that it's a choice. You are no longer reacting and living from old patterns. You are growing, evolving, and making choices from an aligned place. If you chose the old path, promise yourself sometime later that day to either verbally process it with a friend or community member, or reflect in your journal why you made that choice in this situation and what it taught you.

R: REFLECT ON THE TRIGGER

Chances are there is a pattern to be found in the instances when you fall out of alignment. Ask yourself a critical question in these moments: *What pulled me out of alignment?* The answer can help you identify the cause so you'll be better prepared in the future. Was it stress? Too much caffeine? Overwhelm? Not feeling great? Or simply an old habit resurfacing? Your answer will help you gain clarity on what needs your attention.

A: ACCEPT WITH GRACE

Falling off track doesn't mean you have failed; it means you're human. Accepting these moments and giving yourself grace allows you to be gentle with yourself through the growth process and empowers you to dust yourself off and try again. Remember, you're learning! This is new. Would we ever shame a toddler learning to walk for falling on his bum? Or would we know it's a very important part of the process? Give yourself grace while you're taking these important first steps in your new life.

C: CHOOSE AGAIN

We don't need to wait until Monday, the first of the month, or the New Year to start fresh. Every single moment is an opportunity to start again. We fail ourselves when we push to tomorrow what can be done today. Did you freak out and flip off the driver next to you? Play it all out in your head for the next few miles by going back to one of your tools. Breathe, put your hand on your heart, ask what you need, perhaps giggle at what a loony tune you just were and start fresh. Do it now, not tomorrow. You'll be so grateful you did. The key is, don't force it, don't rush, and don't fake it. This isn't about toxic positivity. This is about creating space for ourselves. Feel it, move through it, use a tool, and then start fresh.

T: TRUST THE PROCESS

Remember, growth isn't always linear. It is more often a winding path with ups, downs, and plateaus. If you looked at typical growth on a line graph, it wouldn't be a straight upward trend, but rather peaks, dips, and moments of leveling off. Growth often comes in waves, and setbacks are an indicator of near-future upward momentum. These are opportunities to gather energy before a big upward leap.

I: INTEGRATE THE LESSON

What did this moment and experience teach you? Every time we have a setback, we have access to valuable insight. We just need to create space to integrate it. Instead of locking this experience away because you're ashamed of it, lean in and use it to reinforce your new habits and belief systems. Let it be your reminder that you no longer want to live from a misaligned and disconnected space. Again, be sure to set out time for either verbally processing this with a friend who is supportive of your growth or journaling and processing it on your own. Ask questions of yourself in theta and then journal whatever comes through to you in alpha.

C: CELEBRATE PROGRESS

Be sure to acknowledge how far you have come. Even needing to realign a hundred times is a sign of major growth. Remember, in the past you distracted yourself out of these feelings, kept moving forward amid the resistance, and chose to squash it all below the surface. Every time you are aware of your actions and behaviors, whether you are in or out of alignment, you are winning. Progress deserves celebration. Recognizing your big and small wins keeps you motivated to keep on keepin' on.

E: EMBODY THE SHIFT

Truly living in alignment isn't just about knowing your values and intentions, it's about living them. Embodying this shift means showing up in your life in ways that reflect who you truly are, even in the smallest and most seemingly insignificant moments. It's about progression, not perfection.

Here are some great indicators that illustrate how you are changing in different areas of your life, even in small ways:

- **In Your Morning Routine:** Instead of rushing right from the moment you wake, take at least five minutes to connect, ground, and just be with yourself, whether this involves breathing, journaling, slowly sipping your warm beverage while you daydream, or any other nonactive activity that feels good. Remember theta? This is her time! These few moments set the tone for a regulated nervous system throughout our day. Ever notice when your day starts off chaotic, it just goes from bad to worse? You wake up late, stub your toe on your bed, you're out of toothpaste, you spill coffee on your shirt on the way out the door, AND get stuck in traffic?! Well, what if you knew you had more control and could help dictate the way your day went by setting the tone from the get-go? By taking a few moments of intentional alignment in the morning, we plant the seeds of calm and contentment for the day. We start our day with calm control, accessing the power of theta, and increasing the chance that we will find that place again later. This primes us for responding rather than reacting to our day.

- **In Your Relationships:** You embody alignment and connection by speaking up for yourself when you need to exercise a boundary. You realize that doing so from a place of calm connection yields the best results. Use your tools learned in previous chapters to access a calm, connected place before communicating, as it will yield better results. In any conflict, we can choose to react, causing more tension, chaos, and strife, or we can take whatever time needed to get out of our heads and into our hearts and bodies, back into the present moment, and address the situation from alignment. Look back at Chapter 8 to be reminded of the power of getting into your heart and what activities you can engage in to do so. It's okay to take your time before responding to someone. It also illustrates to them that they can do the same. Operating from a clear head and strong heart is the best starting place for communication!

- **In Your Work Life:** Rather than pushing through stress, burnout, and overwhelm, you take the opportunity to engage in small moments of connection with yourself, whether it be by pausing for some good breathing, getting in nature for a few moments, or reading a few pages of a good book. You are aware of beta's need for a break and so you tap into theta and alpha throughout your day. Beta is your runner, and she can only complete a marathon if you give her the chance to take a few water breaks throughout the event. These don't take long, but they are key to success. Throughout your day, give yourself mini breaks to step out of your busy brain and into your heart and body. Get in nature, take some deep breaths, put your phone on "do not disturb" or leave it behind, daydream, eat lunch in peace. These small moments make all the difference in how we feel during and at the end of our day. Remember, we're still getting it all done, we're just shifting how we *be* while we *do* it all.

- **In Your Self-Talk:** You practice forgiveness, compassion, and giving yourself grace. You focus on progress—not perfection—and you carve out space for integration, whether it be in verbally processing with a friend or journaling through your experiences. You take the time to mine for the answers that you have within, reconnecting with your ego in order to access your whole self.

- **In Your Health and Well-Being:** You are more comfortable saying no to events, people, and environments that no longer serve you. You are leaning into what feels good, and your nervous system is benefiting. You feel less scattered, chaotic, and conflicted than you have in the past.

- **In Your Daily Choices:** You realize that small choices add up. Whether it's being more aware of the content you consume, how you spend your free time, or who you are choosing to be around, you are making more of your choices from a place of authenticity and alignment. Although you are still very much aware of the people around you, you are choosing to put your needs first in more of these situations and decisions because you are now fully realizing the influence it has on how you feel and how you show up for your loved ones.

- **In Your Response to Challenges:** When life throws you a curveball, you are more comfortable with responding from a place of alignment rather than *reacting* from an old script and programming. You are aware of your choices. If you are triggered by criticism or your child has a meltdown, rather than bursting out and reacting, you pause, take a breath, get aligned, and then respond . . . at least most of the time. And when you don't—refer back to the PRACTICE acronym.

I realize it all sounds too good to be true. We can fail? That's okay? Failure is still growth? *What?* The truth is—yes! I am well-versed in this because I have failed, gotten back up, failed again, and continued to live and practice this myself. I'd like to say that now, nearly 99 percent of the time I am fully aware of what I am doing, the choices I am making, and how I am responding. And most of the time, I do so from a place of alignment. The times when I don't, I am fully aware. Even more so if my moment of misalignment happens in front of others—especially my children. These times are particularly painful, as I have not only failed myself but failed to model healthy behavior for them.

BEFORE I HAD THE LANGUAGE . . .

I don't remember exactly what day it was, but I remember the energy.

I was fresh out of school, working at someone's office, running full tilt from the second I opened my eyes. Tired but caffeinated. Stuck in traffic. Furious at slow drivers, closed lanes, everything in my way. My mind was racing ahead, but my body was already drained. I was living in a loop of speed and reaction and didn't even know it had a name.

I stopped to run a quick errand at the store before work. The woman at the checkout was moving slowly—too slowly for my frantic system—and I snapped. I don't even remember what I said. But I know it was sharp, fast, and disconnected.

And here's the part that still lives in my nervous system:
She didn't match my energy.
She didn't defend herself or smile politely.
She just looked at me.
Present. Grounded. Awake.
Her stillness wasn't passive. It was powerful.

And in that moment, I saw myself clearly—misaligned, chaotic, not even in the moment I was living.

That was a turning point.

Because when someone is rooted in alignment, they don't need to say a word.

Their presence holds up a mirror.

And sometimes, that's the exact reflection we need.

I remember one day, not so long ago, when I fell out of alignment in a major way. My husband was traveling for work, which meant that all three kids were wholly my responsibility. I was juggling the morning, trying to do things right, even though I knew it would be a challenge. I woke up early to do my grounding time but somehow got pulled into checking work e-mails. I was making breakfast for the kids while noticing that none of them had gotten dressed yet, when one of them announced they had forgotten to do their homework. The garbage was full and I had to remind my son, yet again, that it was his job to take it out. My other son didn't want what I was making for breakfast but also didn't know exactly what he *did* want. We needed to be out the door in five minutes, so of course two of the kids started to pick on each other, their noise level escalating. The kitchen not only looked like a bomb had gone off, but there was also one inside of me with the fuse burning down.

I exploded.

"I can't take this!" I yelled. "I need garbage out, and food in your mouth. You will eat what I made. You will finish your homework, brush your teeth, and be cleaned up and out the door in two minutes!"

I could literally see them all freeze, tighten, and be impacted by my stress. Was it warranted? Maybe. They weren't listening or doing what I had asked of them, so I lost my cool. Could I have done it from a better place, been firm, direct, to the point, and gotten them to do what they needed to do, and stayed in alignment? Definitely.

At that moment, there was a pause, one that was long enough for me to see the effect I had on them—and I didn't like it. I stopped, took a breath, closed my eyes, sank my head, and then asked myself what I needed to feel my best. First thought—a vacation! Which was not a realistic thought. My second thought was that I needed to make this feel better for all of us. I breathed, connected to myself for a moment, came back to my body, picked my head up, and calmly but firmly spoke to my children.

"I'm one person, and we all need to carry our own weight in the morning so we can get out the door in time. I lost my cool, and that's not your fault, but I need you to do what is required when I ask. The mornings are busy, and we don't have a lot of wiggle room. I know I just lost my temper. I didn't like how that felt, and I'm sure you didn't either. You didn't make me feel that way. I did. All that stress and energy that just came out of me, that's mine, not yours. I'm going to take a moment to myself and breathe while you guys finish your tasks because I need it. Can we all work together to get this done and get out the door on time?"

I took that pause to get back in alignment. My explosion could have resulted in an entire downward spiral for everyone in my family. The day was not only course corrected, I also role modeled for my children some very important things:

- It's okay to lose yourself
- Nobody is responsible for your state except for you
- There are tools that help get you back, and it's okay to ask for space so you can access them

I can't tell you how much switching and reframing moments like this has done for me and my family. It's one of the most subtle yet life-changing, cycle-breaking, generational pivots you can ever make for your lineage. When a woman heals, she doesn't just heal herself—she empowers those who come after. Her transformation creates a ripple effect that touches her family, her community, and ultimately, the world.

HOLDING ALIGNMENT

> ## QUESTIONS & PRACTICES
>
> Every time we fall short and slip into old patterns, it's not a failure—it's a beautiful opportunity for growth. Next time it happens to you, next time you make the choice to enact old patterns by snapping at someone, or showing up in a way that you aren't so proud of, take time to ask yourself these questions:
>
> 1. What is it about that situation that bothered me? What did I do or say that I am not proud of?
>
> 2. If I could go back and try again, what would I want it to look and feel like?
>
> 3. In the future how can I ensure a different outcome? What tools can I implement to set myself up for success?
>
> 4. What did this experience teach me about my new way of life? How can I learn from what happened in order to do better next time?

CHAPTER 12

It's Not Selfish, It's Self-WITH

If there is one thing that keeps people—particularly women—from prioritizing themselves, it's the idea that doing so is selfish. The moment you stop to finally put your feet up, rest for a moment, or take time for yourself, an uncomfortable feeling creeps in. We ask ourselves if we're taking time from others, if there is something someone else needs, or a task that we're ignoring that could benefit someone else. You might experience this so often that you've actually forgotten what it is that you used to do with your free time before you had a career, a household to run, or a spouse and children.

An inner voice creeps up that asks what you think you're doing. How dare you do something for yourself when there are dishes in the sink? This voice believes that if you're not being a martyr, you're not doing it right. It may sound like your mother, grandmother, friend, or someone who you've noticed *doesn't* have dirty dishes in the sink, ever. The voice may even sound like you, but it's important to remember that it's not your whole self speaking; it's an aspect of you that has processed all the societal messages instructing you to do it all, do it better, and be sure to smile and look nice while doing it.

It's easy to listen to this voice, to fall back into the familiar so-called comfort of pushing yourself to a breaking point in order to serve others. As we've talked about, what's familiar is comfortable, even if it's slowly wearing you down into exhaustion. Unfortunately, for a lot of us, exhaustion itself might even feel comfortable. Falling into bed at night, completely empty and unable to cope, can masquerade as accomplishment, even as it drains you. Learning to stay in alignment means learning to identify why that voice—and the concepts it endorses—are in service to no one and nothing.

Imagine for a moment that you are standing in front of a massive building, a structure built brick by brick, each brick representing your belief that self-care is selfish. This tower didn't just appear overnight; it was carefully constructed over time with each new interaction, uncomfortable experience, and expectation of others adding yet another layer to its height, until it reaches so high into the sky that you can't see the top.

The ground was broken for the foundation of this building when you were a child. You were praised for being a good girl, so helpful, so caring of others, so dutiful and kind. While it wasn't said in so many words, you were discouraged from expressing your own needs and desires, which reinforced the idea that selflessness was the path to follow, the one where you put everyone else before yourself.

The first few floors were constructed as you watched your mom, your aunt, or other women in your life put everyone's needs above their own, wearing a cloak of exhaustion as their badge of honor. *This is just what women do,* you may have silently thought to yourself. It's possible these women prided themselves on their ability to circumvent their own needs, perhaps even announcing at the end of the day everything they had done . . . and making it very clear that none of it had been in service to themselves. This was sacrifice. This was the job of a woman.

Then, middle floors were erected as you grew into a young adult and began to experience that saying no came with guilt. You realized that prioritizing yourself often meant disappointing someone else, and that didn't feel good. You'd traversed the floors underneath you, where you'd learned from external sources that serving others was your role, and this was only reinforced internally as you climbed upward through life, feeling the swell of guilt when you let someone else down. Your formative years were spent absorbing the messaging so intently that now the call was coming from inside the house. The voice dismantling your needs and wants was no longer someone else's—it was your own.

Then the top layers, penthouses, and rooftop were added on through societal messaging, reinforcing the glorification of the selfless and self-sacrificing woman. She does it all, doesn't ask for help, and doesn't take breaks to nourish herself. She is a woman who makes sure everyone else comes first, be it friends, family, co-workers, spouse, or children. That's the model of true femininity: absolute selflessness.

This structure of your beliefs stands firm and tall; you no longer even need to see it to believe it. You no longer question its existence; rather, it has become your guiding post for many of your daily decisions and your North Star on the compass when at a crossroads of serving others or yourself. You'll most often choose the path that is reinforced by the thousands of decisions you made climbing each step of this building, each one of them asking you to give a little bit more.

But here is the powerful truth. Just because this structure is tall and mighty does not mean it's unshakable. What if it's all an illusion? What if this is a structure *you* built based on outdated programming and subconscious scripting from your mother, father, teachers, and preachers? Since you built it, you can knock it down. Grab your wrecking ball of truth and prepare to shatter this illusion.

But first let's understand why we have put so much power in this outside belief system rather than in our own truth. You may not even know what your own truth is yet, but together we're going to excavate it because when you can build your own foundation, one in which you can place your full confidence, it will help keep you realigned as you continue down the path of becoming your whole self, one that isn't selfish but realizes that the goal is to be self-*with*.

LOOKING FOR ANSWERS OUTSIDE OURSELVES

For so long we have been conditioned to believe that much of our power and everything we need for happiness and validation exists outside of us. We believe that control over our lives and the sense of achievement it brings comes from managing everything *but us*. It's no wonder then that when life gets busy and chaotic, we lose our footing.

You know what those moments when you slip feel like. You might be feeling gross because of an interaction that didn't go so well with a loved one or co-worker. Maybe you received an e-mail that threw you totally off-kilter. Or maybe you just got cut off in traffic by a guy who you're pretty sure is the same one who was tailgating you just moments before. An ugly feeling rises up. Frustration and anger brew, and we look for a place to assign blame. Maybe your friend is self-centered or that driver is a jerk. Maybe your co-worker doesn't understand the importance of a deadline, or the e-mail you received totally had a snippy tone. It's an attractive and easy option to find a host of reasons why other people are the problem, why something that happened *outside* of you is what has knocked you out of alignment.

And how do we make ourselves feel better when things like this happen? By reaching for something *outside* of ourselves for relief. It feels great in the moment to yell horrible things about that driver, complain to another co-worker that someone else isn't doing their job, or shoot back a snappy e-mail. Even if you don't indulge in lashing out, you might instead go for a quick dopamine hit that will momentarily make you feel better. Hopping on TikTok, scrolling socials, grabbing a coffee, or downing a glass of wine all feel like valid forms of relief when we've been knocked off-kilter and are desperately craving stability.

This *outward* projection, reinforced through our society and culture, leaves us disconnected from our one true source of real power—ourselves. Let's look at how deeply this outside model has shaped our lives and the way in which we move through the world. This is really important to understand as this is part of the foundational principles that are going to help you truly lean into the time with yourself that you need, deserve, and crave.

External Validations

1. **Distractions:** In times of discomfort or chaos, you reach for external distractions rather than internal stability—and, wow, is the modern world absolutely full of them! When life feels like too much, you reach for things that temporarily dull the discomfort but do nothing to solve the root cause. You are putting bandages on bullet wounds

when you scroll, binge-watch, overeat, shop, or reach for caffeine or perhaps some alcohol. You are only just prolonging the pain and discomfort, seeking easy, temporary refuge.

2. **Giving Our Power Away:** You base your sense of worth on how well you meet expectations, either other people's or unrealistic ones you've set for yourself. If someone isn't giving you praise, thanking you for helping them, or constantly congratulating all of your efforts, you may feel less than accomplished. And when the day ends, you may not really know where the inner hollowness comes from. The truth is that there is no amount of external validation that can patch this big of a hole. Only you can do that for yourself.

3. **Outdated Models of Self-Care:** In keeping with the societal norm of seeking external validation, you've been sold a self-care philosophy that is based on achieving relief through buying something, booking an appointment, or escaping your life for a moment or a weekend. True change occurs when you realize that self-care only comes from true self-connection. It's an inside job that requires the ability to say no to everything and everyone else, if only for a few moments, and say yes to yourself.

BECOMING SELF-WITH

When the system fails, we blame ourselves. How many self-help books have you read only to find yourself back in the same stuck situations and circumstances you had hoped to change? You assume you are the failure. You blame yourself, then distract yourself with an easy *external* source rather than realizing it's not your fault. The system you have been sold is broken. The power has never been in any of those things. It's *always* been in you. And knowing that is where everything starts to change.

You've learned how in the previous chapters. You've got the keys to making this happen. But, of course, there will still be those moments when you lose yourself because of an external stressor. Your heart rate escalates, your jaw clenches, your neck and shoulders get tight, and your mind starts racing. It's in these moments, not the escapes to the spa, that you can save yourself from the pain. You know exactly how to return to yourself, your core, your alignment in an instant. The key to staying in alignment is in shifting from no longer being *selfless* and instead taking time each day, if only a few moments, to be self-*with*.

Becoming self-with ensures that you are no longer relying on the outside world to dictate how you feel. You no longer require the perfect conditions, mood, or approval of others in order to give yourself permission to pause. You no longer put your time at the bottom of your very long to-do list. You put it at the top. Because when you take care of yourself first, everything else changes.

Let's create a fun system around this because putting your attention and intention on getting self-with creates an inner foundation with deep roots of connection and alignment that allow you to show up fully, no matter what is going on around you. This is where true power resides. Not in how well you keep it all together, not in how many items you somehow seamlessly juggle, not in how much you can give to others, but in how deeply you are connected to yourself.

Shifting from an outside-in model to an inside-out way of living and getting self-with is where everything changes. Being self-with doesn't need to take a lot of time. It's realizing the importance and making space for even just five minutes of being with yourself. I suggest taking five first thing in the morning and five just before going to bed to implement this time. Remember those brain waves? The morning and evening are when we're in theta; our subconscious door is open, and anything we do here becomes a new habit more quickly. Taking the time in the evening sets you up for a good night's rest, which will directly impact how your day starts tomorrow! Those five minutes at the beginning and end of the day will help keep you aligned—and get you realigned when you backslide.

You may be wondering how such a small amount of time can have such a great impact, but try it for a week or two and refer to this Self-With Checklist to remind yourself of the benefits of setting aside just five minutes at the beginning and end of the day.

THE SELF-WITH CHECKLIST

The Self-With Checklist is a way to remind you of what you're actually doing here. Rather than allowing old programming to make us feel guilty about putting our needs higher up on our list, the Self-With Checklist leverages how powerful taking these five minutes is—not just in shifting our lives, but the lives of everyone around us as well. I recommend writing it out and sticking it on your mirror, in your car, or somewhere you will see it often. The goal of this is to remind you in those moments where you used to make the old choice, to PAUSE and PRACTICE this new path.

Being Self-With isn't selfish. Being Self-With:

S: Sustains you–Taking this time for you isn't indulgent. It's a necessity of being human. Just like your phone or computer needs to be charged in order to continue to perform, you also need to restore your own energy in order to function at your best.

E: Elevates others–When you take time to prioritize yourself, you show up differently. It will lead to more present, engaged, and compassionate interaction with everyone around you. A well-nourished version of you benefits more than just you. It touches everyone in your life.

L: Leads by example–By setting boundaries and taking the time and initiative to take care of yourself, you inspire and empower others to do the same. Our actions speak louder than words, and through your actions, you're showing others that taking time for yourself is healthy.

F: Fosters true connection–When you move through life from a place of exhaustion, your relationships become an obligation rather than a choice or pleasure. Taking care of yourself first allows you to connect from presence and fulfillment rather than depletion.

W: Worthy of rest–Rest is no longer something you feel the need to earn. No more days spent running around checking off all the things so that you can finally take the rest you deserve. You can revel in the knowledge that you are worthy of rest simply because you exist.

I: Invites growth–Connection with yourself is a gateway to growth and alignment. Creating space in time for self-reflection, introspection, tuning in, and getting reacquainted with your desires and taking action to fulfill them breaks old patterns and allows you to truly step into your whole self.

T: Takes nothing away–This isn't an either/or equation, it's both/and. You are not choosing either them *or* you; you are choosing both them *and* yourself. This helps reframe that taking care of yourself does not imply denying others' needs, but rather enhances your ability to help others because you now show up as your whole self instead of giving from whatever is left over after constant overextension.

H: Heals generational patterns–This one is my personal favorite. You're doing it differently this time around, and you're showing others how! By prioritizing self-connection, you break the cycle for all the little girls and women who come from us and after us. They will no longer see self-sacrifice as love or a badge of honor. The new way forward includes caring for yourself in the equation.

EXERCISES & ACTIVITIES

Take some time this week and check in with yourself before you get out of bed. Connect with your thoughts. What comes up for you? A really powerful exercise is to start listening to the subconscious questions you are asking yourself when you first wake up. The way you do this is to sit with yourself and follow where your thoughts go. The questions we tend to ask ourselves as women can include, but aren't limited to:

- Who needs me?
- How will I get it all done?
- How can I best serve everyone?

- Will they like me?
- Am I good enough?

Another great thing to pay attention to in the morning is asking yourself what feelings you are addicted to. What situations do you find or create that feed this addiction?

- Are you addicted to stress?
- Chaos?
- Anxiousness?
- Busyness?

I never realized until I took part in this quick check-in that I was addicted to stress. I would wake up and not really feel awake and ready for the day until I found that feeling of stress. I felt unsteady and ungrounded. Looking back, I realize that often when I woke, I felt contentment in my dreamy state but it was unfamiliar so I pulled myself out of it by finding external situations to feed my stress addiction. Remember when we learned that you will choose known pain over unknown possibilities? That's what I was doing.

I didn't feel like myself until I checked my e-mail. I'd scroll past the good ones or the junk mail ones—and go right to any conflicts, any challenge at work, any e-mails that answered the question *who needs me? What am I missing out on? What am I behind on?* If that didn't work, I'd lightly scroll the news apps or socials to see if there were any conflicts going on in the world, politics, or local news (spoiler—there always is) in order to have something to feed that internal pull, that need for stress in order to feel like I was awake and functioning. Then, I'd get into a heated discussion with my husband about . . . well, just about anything! The coffee maker, the weather, my body, the kids' schedules, that work challenge—it goes on and on. Does any of this sound familiar? When we start to realize we are using these external circumstances to feed an internal addiction, we can start to change things. Awareness is the first step, and creating a different home to connect to is what changes that. In order to shift our perspective from the outside world, we need to create a connection with our internal world.

My mornings are now very different. When I wake up, the first question I *choose* to ask myself is something like, *What is it that I need today? What would make this day feel more fun? Light? Free? Joyful?* And then I spend some time getting to the bottom of that question. If I choose to go on socials early, I get clear on why I'm going on, so it's not simply mindless scrolling and allowing an outside source to dictate how I feel. Most importantly, I don't let it set my tone for the day.

Are there still days when I wake up feeling overwhelmed, stressed, a lot out of tune? One hundred percent, yes! But the difference is now I know what I can do to get out of it, and I know what choices I can make that will keep me in it. It's a choice. It's in my hands. No external situations have the power over me. I have found my power within.

CHAPTER 13

Creating Inner Beacons

We've talked a lot about external stressors, all of the elements of the outside world that carry a lot of power in our society. If there's one thing I want you to take from this book, it's the idea that the answer to connecting with your whole self lies inside you, an eternal wellspring of power, not in some outside source that will only be temporary. With that in mind, a great way to stay in alignment is to create some inner beacons that you can use as touchstones as you move through this new life, where you don't simply exist to serve others.

What is an inner beacon? An inner beacon is your internal light. It's a place to come home to when things get chaotic, when life gets messy. In order to start practicing letting go of external circumstances, to stop allowing things outside of us to dictate and control us, we need to establish these internal anchors.

Picture this: You are all jazzed up from reading this book. You're ready to *pause* and *practice* carving a new path for yourself. This time when your boss puts more work on you, or a friend rubs you the wrong way, you are going to

CREATING INNER BEACONS

handle it differently. You're going to stop giving the outside things power over you. So, you gear up, you pep talk yourself throughout the day, awaiting the opportunity to try out this new system.

Then it happens. Someone cuts you off, work gets stressful, and you make the conscious decision to not allow all your emotions, feelings, and self-worth to be tethered to this moment. You cut the cord. But now what?! Now you're sitting here with nowhere to go . . . and the truth is that it might be really uncomfortable. You stood up to your boss, you turned your back on a so-called friend who always takes but never gives, you gave your child space to work through things on their own while you sat by their side. In other words—you did it! But how many yucky thoughts came up while you did? Things like, am I doing this right? What do I do now? What did the book say to do next? This doesn't feel like it's working!

This is why many self-help techniques fail. You rely on the next steps hand delivered by the author, the checklist that was created to get you through moments exactly like this one. But you can't remember what comes next, and you can't access that bullet-pointed list in the moment . . . so you feel like you've failed yet again. Maybe you become frustrated. Maybe you give up.

This is different. Why? Because you don't need to be connected to me in order to make this system work—you only need to be connected to *you*! You have instant access to your best teacher; you have your guru and mentor on speed dial. Through establishing your inner beacon, all you need to do in the craziest of situations is come back to your home, your center. Every time you do, it will feel more familiar, more comfortable, and your own voice will become louder and more clear. You learn to pause, take a breath to connect, to get you out of your head and into your body and heart. You ask yourself: *What is it that I need at this moment?* By continuing to use the tools in The Connection Code chapter, your toolbox will expand and so will your connection to *you*.

Asking yourself what *you* need when your child is melting down isn't selfish. It gets you back to a place from where you can be helpful. Grounding yourself through breathing or rooting your feet into the ground during a tense interaction—instantly getting you out of your mind and back into your body—has the power to create connection from the chaos and conflict. You get to choose. It's your time, it's your turn to take that power back and let it positively influence every person you come into contact with.

Think of your inner beacon as a light in a lighthouse or a flame. We feed it every day. We continue adding a bit of kindling so that when we need to access this inner light, the fire is there, burning brightly. I like to visualize the inner flame in tough moments, and I visualize my breath giving the flame strength. Just like blowing on a fire makes it bigger, I use my breath in crazy situations to strengthen my inner fire and get reconnected to my power within. It's a great visual. It calms, centers, and strengthens me. That's a pretty epic combo!

We strengthen that fire through our daily rituals and practices so that when game time comes, we're ready. And we continue to *practice* . . . which, as we all know, doesn't always make perfect. There will be times when you do this and it doesn't go the way you hoped, but remember, this isn't about perfection. This is about progression. And every time you choose this new path, you are rewiring your brain and rewriting your story.

We will talk about how to light our inner beacons in a moment, but first let's discuss how we dim them and the contributing factors that try to put your fire out!

SELF-DOUBT:

Perhaps you have something bold you have always wanted to do. But every time you think of taking action or a step toward this ideal future, self-doubt creeps in. I have no time. My life is too busy. I don't know how. If I fail, everyone will judge me. Even though your intuition, your gut, your inner beacon, and whole self are nudging you to take a courageous step forward, you talk yourself out of it, convincing yourself you'll fail before you even try.

Self-doubt makes you second-guess your intuition. It negates that powerful gut feeling and instead leads you to keep listening to your cautious *rational* brain. Instead of trusting your inner guide, you let fear and potential outside judgments hold you back. In doing so, you let the flame weaken, taking it down to the smallest flicker.

PAST EXPERIENCES:

Maybe in the past you've opened yourself up and vulnerably shared a dream, goal, wish, or personal struggle . . . and it didn't go so well. You were judged, discouraged, or you were hurt. So you learned that building walls around your heart, your true desires and needs, was a way to stay safe. Later, even in those moments when you feel called to share and feel that flicker of a fire in your belly, you hold back, play small, and stay quiet.

Putting walls around our hearts doesn't protect us. These walls keep us stuck in a familiar hell, playing small, never truly living out our calling. Your inner guidance is whispering to you to go for it, but you shove it down, quiet it in order to avoid getting hurt.

EVERYDAY LIFE:

You wake up, check your phone, e-mails, socials, take care of all the needs of the household. You rush out the door to get the kids to school and yourself to work, respond to text messages, and do everything necessary in order to keep the wheel of life turning for that day. You finally get to the end of your day and feel drained and disconnected. You haven't had a single moment to yourself—or maybe you just chose to anchor to outside forces instead, as per usual. Your flame flickers.

Constant stimulation pours water on your inner light. When you're always reacting to and tuned in to the outside world, you can't even hear your inner voice. Over time, this contributes to feeling lost, unfulfilled, or completely unsure of what you truly desire.

Of course the world is absolutely full of all kinds of things that dim our inner beacon, and we're actively participating in some of them. The list below is just a handful of examples, as well as an offered reframe or shift. Which ones resonate with you?

- You look for reassurance before making decisions
    - ✷ Shift: You practice trusting that your inner knowing is enough. Before seeking outside advice or validation, pause and ask: *What do I already know to be true?*
- You question your worth if not shown approval by others
    - ✷ Shift: Your worth isn't up for debate! Instead of asking, *Do they approve of me/this?*, try *Do I approve of me/this?*
- You change your mind based on the opinions of others

- ✳ Shift: Ask yourself, *How do I actually feel about this?* before hearing others' opinions or letting them influence your decisions
- You define yourself through your to-dos and accomplishments
  - ✳ Shift: You are worthy as you are, not just for what you produce. Practice stillness and acknowledgment without attaching it to external achievements or to-dos.
- You feel unworthy if any of these roles change. For example, your child no longer needs you to tie their shoes, or the big project at work is all wrapped up.
  - ✳ Shift: Build self-worth in WHO you are, not just in what you do for others
- You let the emotions of others dictate how you feel
  - ✳ Your energy is your responsibility. Before absorbing anyone else's emotions, ask: *Is this mine or theirs?* If not yours, release it. I add a physical cue and visual for myself by unhooking it from me and hooking it back onto them or blowing it away like I'm making a wish on a dandelion.
- You absorb negative energy from acquaintances, family members, and the media.
  - ✳ Shift: Ask yourself, *Is this mine to carry?* If not, take it off! I visualize unhooking something from me and blowing it away like dandelion fuzz. Extra bonus if you make a wish for yourself or the world!
- You find yourself consuming disempowering information, such as the news and politics

- * Shift: Protect what you consume. Be intentional before jumping into any news source or social media. Ask: *What is my intention? How do I want to feel, and is this the best use of my time?* This creates a moment of pause and an opportunity to check in if this choice is aligned.
- You surround yourself with people who discredit your intuition or judge your growth
  - * Shift: Spend more time with expanders, not limiters. The people meant for you will celebrate your growth and respect your boundaries. As you continue to step into your power, more people from your tribe will show up in your life!
- You feel responsible for *fixing* other people
  - * Shift: Release the fixer role. Nobody is broken. Instead of asking, *How can I help fix this/them?*, reframe to *How can I hold space for this without carrying it/taking it on?*
- You mold your energy to fit the needs of others
  - * Shift: Your energy is intended to be fully yours. Before adjusting yourself to match someone else, ask *Am I shrinking to fit or standing in my truth?*
- You make choices based on external *shoulds* rather than internal alignments
  - * Shift: Drop the *shoulds* and follow your soul. Reconnect to you, your goals, your wants, your desires, and your inner wisdom through journaling, stillness, listening, and

daydreaming. Turn off outside sources and voices during your car rides and morning time. Listen to you. The more you honor what truly lights you up, the more aligned, joyful, and easy your life becomes.

Ready for some good news? Your inner beacon never goes away. It's always there, no matter how dim, just waiting for you to come tend to it. Like a lighthouse, it will always be there to guide you. And like a lighthouse, it exists precisely to guide you through even the worst of storms. The way we strengthen the flame isn't by doing more, it's by doing less. We clear the interference, the static, the noise, we slow down, connect with ourselves, pause, breathe, and slowly learn to trust ourselves again.

STRENGTHENING OUR INNER BEACONS

One of the main reasons we have lost connection with our inner beacons is that we have become so focused on our external world. We have forgotten the power of simplicity. Getting the answers we crave is no longer something outside of us; it simply requires presence and a willingness to return to and choose ourselves, over and over again. Luckily, that inner beacon is always there, waiting for you to return. You can find your way back and strengthen your connection to it with some simple practices.

1. *Pause before seeking external guidance and validation.* Before phoning a friend for advice, asking Google, or comparing yourself to what others would do in this situation, simply tune in to yourself. Take a breath and ask yourself, *What do I know to be true? What feels right to me?* Get quiet

long enough to sit with the answer. Perhaps take time to write and reflect in a journal. Then, if you still want to consult outside sources, go for it. If your actions stem from an informed and aligned place, you've got the right foundation to make good decisions—the foundation of yourself.

2. *Get comfortable with being uncomfortable.* Practice sitting with and breathing through uncomfortable feelings rather than distracting yourself from them. Growth happens in the space between the stimulus and reaction. The power is in the pause, because that is where you make a conscious choice. You decide whether or not to follow the path that has been paved for you, the one paved from conditioning, scripting, and false beliefs. Next time you're feeling yucky and perhaps catch yourself turning to a numbing agent like social media, food, or Netflix, ask yourself, *What is this moment here to teach me?* Sit with it until you hear your answer. Again, I highly recommend writing these down. Journaling gives you an anchor, a place, and a way to practice hearing your voice.

3. *Listen to your inner whispers.* Don't assume these revelations come as big wake-up calls. The power is in the subtle nudges, the quiet voice that is so easily drowned out by life's noise. The one that whispers, *It's time for a break now, this doesn't feel good in my body.* Let's wait before sending that e-mail, let's breathe so we can respond rather than react. Transfer that voice to real situations by saying out loud, "I'm going to need a minute to sit with this before responding." It's in these moments that we win.

CREATING INNER BEACONS

4. *Make choices based on what aligns with you.* Each time you make choices for yourself, rather than what you believe you *should* do or what others are doing, you strengthen your inner certainty. You flex the muscle of change, and although it's perhaps a bit uncomfortable at first, it becomes easier and easier to access. Soon, it becomes second nature and feels clear, connected, and confident. With every aligned choice you make, your inner fire becomes stronger, always making it easier and easier for you to find your way home amid the storm.

The more you choose you, the more you feed your inner beacon, the more you fan your inner flame, the less you will need to reach for strength outside of you. In those tricky moments, you will no longer be trying to remember what that book said about parenting with presence. Rather, you'll start to realize that the best teacher, the greatest adviser, is and has always been within. You will know that your inner beacon is strengthening when:

- You trust yourself to navigate the hard moments without going to external sources.
- You no longer feel lost or thrown off balance when things get crazy because you know where to go and how to get there.
- You truly believe that the most powerful guide isn't someone else. It's the voice inside of you that has always been there, just waiting for you to listen.

Your inner beacon will never leave you. It will never judge or abandon you. It will never be unavailable to pick up that call when you need it most, or leave you searching in the dark. You've got her on speed dial and in your back pocket.

It's yours. Always and forever. All you've got to do to access it is turn inward and listen.

ACCESSING INNER BEACONS IN REAL LIFE

One of the places I most often use these tools is for school pickup. While my kids are at school, I am very much riding my beta waves, getting it all done and being a go-getter. Whether I'm writing content, filming material, in back-to-back meetings, or creating a podcast script, I am in go-go mode all day.

Yet, I want to be in a different state when I pick up our three kids. Although they attend an incredible school where they learn breathwork as well as nervous system and emotional regulation, they still have held it together all day. They need to let it all out when they hop in the car. Ever had that happen to you? You're so excited to see them and hear about their day, but then they each have their own story of their horrible day, are mad that you didn't bring the right car snacks, and were five minutes late or god knows what else. In these moments, driving in Miami traffic with three mini dictators in my car, I can't escape into nature or get on my grounding mat.

In these moments I use my tools. I go to my inner beacon and anchor. I breathe, check in, and ask what I need so I can be present and grounded. I have found that the key is to do this on the way to school pickup. Ideally, I'd have time well before that to take care of myself for an hour or so before pickup. On the rare occasion that I do, I go to the gym, sweat it out, take a shower, and feel like I have literally washed off my work hat and immersed myself in mama mode. Cape switch! But typically, I am running from Zooms and right

CREATING INNER BEACONS

into their pickups. I have about ten minutes in the car to figure this out.

Because I check in with myself often, I instantly get an answer to my question of what I need at the moment. It's often something like *complete quiet*, and so I choose not to return that phone call or catch up on a podcast during the drive. Or, my inner voice says it needs *fun*, so I roll the windows down, put on a chipper song, and sing my heart out. I don't use this time to fit in one more thing or do something that I *should* do. I do what I want, and it makes all the difference in how I show up, not just for me, but for my family too.

Do other people see my hair flying out the windows while I'm scream-singing Taylor Swift? Do they think that I'm a little bit . . . off? Maybe! I don't care. I needed that, and by listening to my inner voice, I tuned in to what was necessary in the moment for me—not for everyone else, and not for society to approve of. Once you have fanned the flames of your inner beacon, that is what will give you a warm, fuzzy feeling all over—not the approval or rejection of others. That's the power and freedom available to you, if you are willing to take a moment, breathe deep, and check in with the best teacher you'll ever have—yourself.

CHAPTER 14

The Path to You: A Road Map for Realignment

I have leveraged the importance of taking care of myself in my life because I saw what happened when I didn't. Remember my story of becoming so ill? I was hit with the double whammy of Lyme disease plus exposure to toxic mold, and I saw my family suffer. I witnessed firsthand what happens when you don't have tools that you can actually regularly use in your life to help stay in alignment, to actually take care of yourself before serving others. I was no longer able to help. Not only that, I became a burden to my family. They never expressed this or did anything to make me feel that way, but I saw that not only could I no longer take care of them, I could barely take care of myself. I couldn't handle the sound of our kids' voices. My brain was so inflamed that the slightest uptick of noise sent me over the edge.

What I typically perceived as their sweet, playful squeals now felt like nails on a chalkboard. If they were all talking at once, it was even worse—like someone was screaming in my ear. And that was just the physical side of it. Emotionally, I had to deal with the guilt and shame of being a mother who flinched at the sound of her own children's laughter. The mornings, with all the moving pieces of getting everyone ready, fed, and out the door, were pure torture for me. Meanwhile, I had people telling me to enjoy every moment, because it all goes so fast. Emotional reactions piled on top of physical pain in a way that was debilitating.

I wasn't able to perform the tag team that my husband and I do, usually without even verbalizing. The dance that happens every morning as we work together to get the kids ready for the day became an insurmountable trudge for me, and my husband lost his dance partner. I could barely open my eyes. Everything just hurt so badly.

Although he never expressed that this was taxing on him, I could feel tension between us. Normally we enjoyed small, precious moments of connection during our morning routine: sustained glances, the flicker of a smile when something played out *exactly* the way one of us had known it would. We had learned to carve out seconds that were just for us in order to feed our relationship while taking care of our kids. But then when I went to lock eyes, his were scanning the room, figuring out his next play. He was living his life ten steps ahead in the way he always had, but now it was clear he was on his own. With no partner to help pick up any pieces, he couldn't let a single detail drop, not only at home, but also in the clinic we had built together over the last decade. He was worried for me and simultaneously overwhelmed.

In the beginning of a relationship, if your partner is coming down with something, you fuss over them, make them soup, remind them to rest, ensure they get what they need in order to recover. Once there are a couple of kids in the mix, your partner's sneeze becomes not a moment of compassion and concern for them, but rather an *oh shit* moment. Your brain plays out a scenario where they are out of commission and you are handling everything by yourself. This was similar. My husband was always there for me during my illness . . . but he also had to be there for everyone else, and there was only so much of him to go around.

Looking back, I can recognize this experience as a great gift because it forced me to figure out ways to take care of myself that were realistic. It made me stop pushing past my breaking point in the busy week when I needed to take a breath but told myself to push through until the weekend. My body was begging for breaks, but I didn't know how to access them during my peak "get shit done" time of the weekday push. I was in all beta, all the time. If I was resting, I wasn't being productive. And if I wasn't being productive, I was letting someone down.

The forms of self-care that had been bought and sold to me required scheduling an appointment at the salon, carving out time for a massage, or some other temporary escape from my life where I could be whisked away for a full hour. When I finally did get to the weekend, guess what? Things popped up. Little chores here. Reminders there. A dust bunny under the bed or a ring around the bathtub let me know that a woman's work was never done. There was also just *one more thing* to do before I could put my manicured feet up, idly relaxing in the perfectly clean and ordered home, while my contented children played, and my husband told me about his week. That certainly sounds nice, and if you examine the picture closely, you'll notice it's the same kind of imagery that is used to sell us on the temporary escapes that are nicely packaged and come with a price tag. You know, the ones that don't work.

If my whole self tried to tell me it was all too much, I just raised the volume on the lie of *one more thing* and the promise of that perfect evening that never actually came to fruition. The few times I did actually listen and was able to somehow carve out some space, it meant putting my to-do list on someone else—asking my husband to help with pickups or make dinner so I could sit for an hour in a massage chair while someone rubbed my feet and nurtured my soul. In reality, what actually happened was that I sat in the chair, iPad in hand, catching up on all the things—e-mails, food planning, social events. These distractions served a dual purpose; I had time and space, so I used them to get through my to-do list in order to feel like an accomplished female, while also putting a buffer between me and the guilty voice that chided me for taking this time when my family needed me. But . . . I could still hear it.

Getting sick forced me to create my Road Map for Realignment, a way to nurture myself as soon as I heard the warning from my whole self, letting me know that we needed a break. I needed tools that were accessible in my busy life. Tools I could actually use in the thick of it without having to get a babysitter, rely on someone else, or push through until I had time to actually listen to what my body was trying to tell me.

This is how *The Connection Code* was born.

It was born out of the spaces and gaps in the self-care model we have all been following. Born out of the need to serve today's woman, the one who was empowered to believe she could do it all, only to realize she doesn't want to, or it's too much. It was created as the solution to burnout, overwhelm, and feeling disconnected from the life we crave and the women we once were. It was created to fill the gap between who we let society tell us to be and who we actually are. A version of us that we have been longing to get back to, maybe without even being consciously aware of it. There's a reason we feel lonely amid the crowd; the yearning to connect with our true self knows that we can't fully engage with others if we aren't integrated with ourselves.

For me this process began slowly. I needed to dip my toes in these new waters; for so long I had heard about incorporating gratitude practice, taking time to breathe or journal, but I honestly never really felt these practices would make an impact. Perhaps I had been conditioned to believe that the subtle isn't impactful, that more is better, that doing less is not going to amount to anything. Underneath it all, I believed that without producing, without *doing*, I was not worthy.

This has been nearly a decade of unlearning, repatterning, noticing, becoming aware, practicing, falling forward, falling short, and getting back up and forgiving myself time and time again. Of doing it out loud. Of speaking out when I don't like how I showed up. Of telling my kids I'm going to try that again. Nearly a decade of practicing saying no and experiencing the terrible fear that it would result in rejection and loss, that my friendship circle would change, or people would push back. I'm here to tell you it does, it will, they might—and that's okay.

You will have vulnerability hangovers from showing up open when you used to be closed. From staying at the table when you would have normally left, not because it wasn't your table, but because you couldn't speak up for what you needed. True growth happens in these moments, the ones where we double down on standing true to what we believe in, even when it's uncomfortable. This doesn't mean joining movements and protests and all of a sudden showing up at every rally to fight for what you believe in—although it can! This standing in your truth is subtle and quietly confident. It's in the seemingly small moments where you choose to pause instead of reacting, taking a moment to check in and ask what *you* need. It's these moments that are your true power.

What is on the other side is a life of joy, freedom, authenticity, and connection with who you truly are. That results in sleeping more soundly at night and rediscovering the love of the person you truly are. It results in others around you being inspired just by witnessing you bloom into the woman you came here to be. It's all worth it. You are worth it, and you're not alone.

We're doing this together.

As I was relearning and forging this new path, it helped me to create systems to follow. Perhaps you, too, have been following a path that no longer works for you. Maybe you have also heard those little whispers from somewhere deep inside of you saying, *I can't!* or *It's too much!* Maybe you stuff them down and keep yourself distracted because you feel there is nothing you can do about them, so you trudge on—just like I did. But at what point will it become too much? When will you hit your edge? Maybe for you it's not Lyme or mold toxicity, but maybe it's a breakdown, disease, burnout, or negative impacts on your relationships with your loved ones. At what point will you look back and wish you could have stopped and taken another track?

I spent over a decade hacking my way through a tangled brush of misalignment, hoping to figure out why I felt so disconnected, why I kept finding myself stuck in old patterns. In the moments where I actually got quiet enough to listen, I heard something inside of me begging for a life that felt like mine. I have tripped over the roots, taken wrong turns, and spent years trying to make sense of patterns that for so long were keeping me stuck. But now, that path has cleared. Not just for me, but for you, and for all of us.

There's a fork in the road, and it's in front of you right now. We've talked about how our ego will keep us sitting with the known, convincing ourselves that being uncomfortable is actually comfortable . . . or at least, better than how unsettling it is to try something new. One of the paths in front of you is paved not with good intentions (although it may feel like it), but with the familiar. It looks like the obvious choice, because the other path is different, strange, even scary. But even though it may not feel like the right choice, it's still a *choice*! Each time you take it, you will rewire and retrain your ego that new isn't scary, different isn't strange. Although the choice is yours, I have tried to make the path a bit easier by forging the way, bushwhacking through the tangle in order to create the systems in this book that ultimately create a new path for all of us. I've marked the way, built the bridge, and created the systems so you don't have to spend a decade figuring it all out.

This is the path back to you. Not the you who has been taught to blend in, to stay quiet, and to play small, but the version of you who is aligned, is fully in your body, and makes choices and decisions from that place. This is the you who listens to that inner voice, your guide, your guru. The *you* who knows exactly how to get back into alignment and inner connection when life happens and you get bumped out. The *you* who stands fully in her power and inspires other women to do the same. The *you* who is clear, connected, and aligned.

The Connection Code is not just a theory or a tool in your toolbox that you pull out and dust off whenever you finally have time at the end of that long week. It's something you live daily, it's a constant decision and reminder to choose yourself, even just for a moment. I know how difficult it is to absorb all the information in this book. I realize that you

THE PATH TO YOU: A ROAD MAP FOR REALIGNMENT

may be saying right now, "But this new path doesn't seem so simple! There are pages and pages of information here for me to remember!" Don't give up now or allow that big sister ego to tell you this is too much to handle. Here are the five key aspects of the Road Map to Realignment that will help build out your day so that you can take care of yourself while continuing to care for others *and* get it all done!

1. **Morning:** Spend at least 5 (but ideally about 20) minutes checking in with yourself before the day begins.
    a. Refer to the Roadmap to Realignment info (in the Resources section) to stay aligned with your brain waves
    b. Use red or amber light as much as possible
    c. The key action step here is to *listen* and then to *journal*

- **Midday Alignment Check-In:** Notice any shifts in energy that might be required and carve out time to incorporate your tools.
    a. Get in nature, take some time for deep breathing, eat lunch away from screens, turn your phone off, go for a walk, get in your body, and take a brain break. Remember your beta waves, your marathon runner? This is her time for a water break. It doesn't have to be long, but it is a really important and powerful move to shift how the rest of your day goes and feels.
    b. This may feel unproductive, yet it's one of the most important things you can do in

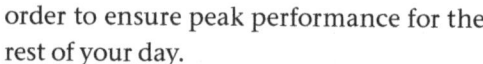

order to ensure peak performance for the rest of your day.

    c. Action step here is to *connect*. Connect with self, connect with others, connect with nature, connect with your heart and your body.

- **Evening Reflection & Rest:** This is where we wash off the day, reassess, and rest.

    a. At least 5 minutes (but ideally 20) spent winding down, emptying your mind, getting into your body and heart while transitioning into a wind-down routine, ensuring quality sleep.

    b. The quality of your day tomorrow starts with the night before

    c. Use the Regulate Your Rhythm brain waves resource as a guide to help you shift out of beta and into alpha, then theta, and then delta when you sleep.

- **Non-Negotiables:** Establish your hard NOs. If you have kids, would you ever let them run in the street?! NO! That is a non-negotiable hard no. What are your hard nos? Aim to establish at least five. This can be anything from no longer answering e-mails after 6 P.M., taking five minutes to yourself in the morning, or no longer saying yes when you really want to say no. I love this acronym for NO: Nourish Oneself. Saying no to something allows you to (finally) say yes to yourself or say no to something you no longer want so you can say "hell yes!" to the things you do.

- **Community & Support:** Having like-minded community and support is crucial, as it helps you know you are not alone in this process. Having other women who are also leaning into their whole selves will remind you to do the same in the moments where you want to cave or fall into old patterns. Having women to lean on when you fall short and feel that you have failed. Having women to remind you that life happens and it's less about what happens and more about how you handle it. You're going to fall down nine times but get up ten—and your community will be there, lending a hand. Having trouble finding your people? Come check out my website and resources to help get you started: drmelissasonners.com.

Choosing ourselves does not mean we are no longer choosing others. The more you start to take time for yourself, the more you are going to realize what a huge impact it has. Imagine pushing through your day when you are fried versus taking a few moments, getting out of your head and into your body and heart, and then moving through your day from that place. Imagine the clarity in decision-making, the presence you will bring to every interaction. We cannot give to others what we can't give to ourselves, and if we want to be fully connected with our loved ones, we must first create that within ourselves.

This is how we do it.
This is how we win.
We get to have both.

REFLECTIVE PROMPTS/EXERCISES:

1. Imagine creating your own road map. What are three small but powerful steps that you could prioritize today?

2. How does showing up for yourself help you show up for others? How will your loved ones benefit from you taking a few moments to regularly connect with yourself?

3. How would your relationships, career, health, and well-being shift if you stopped choosing between yourself and others, and instead embraced both?

CONCLUSION

Congratulations! You've already come a long way just by making the time for yourself required to sit down and read this book. You listened to that voice, recognized the deep sense that you were made for something different, something more than simply making it through your day, checking off the boxes, and surviving this life. You've already decided that the old rinse-and-repeat methods aren't working for you. You've already abandoned the old path, sensing that there is a better way. That was the first step, the one that you took out of exhaustion or perhaps even desperation.

And in many ways, that first step is the hardest one.

You've already started your journey. The journey away from self-doubt and people-pleasing, away from that feeling of disconnection. You can already feel the bright light—your inner beacon—gaining strength just from seeing this new path and recognizing that there are alternatives. You already knew that the old path was not going anywhere good, but now you have found the other route, the new way. It's your turn, and it's time for a change.

But this isn't just any change.

This is a shift in the fabric of not just your life, but all the generations of women that come after you. This is a transformation that spans a limitless number of women, from your daughters to your grandchildren, to your great-grandchildren, and so on. They may not know your name, but something deep inside of them will thank you. Your bloodline has been waiting for a woman like you, one who will shatter paradigms and step outside of the box, one who isn't afraid to feel the pushback, to take risks, and to speak up in order to better not only her own life, but the lives of the women who will follow.

You are ready to step into the role and set the example of the new path, not only finding inner peace but spreading it to those around you. When you do this, you will be met with an invisible set of hands, guidance from your ancestors. The seed that was planted inside of you by the brilliant, sturdy women of the past will flower back into existence, no longer poisoned by the demands of the modern world and the expectations that you have adhered to for so long. The universe will conspire to work in your favor. You will start to notice coincidences and synchronicities. They will show you, whisper to you . . . *keep going this way.*

You are a cycle breaker.

Being a cycle breaker doesn't mean you have all the answers, it simply means you are ready to find them. You trust that many of them are within you, and you are willing to make a commitment to hear and nurture the voice expressing them. It's a daily choice, a decision to move through life differently. You have opened your ears, and you can't stop listening to what is and has always been there. Your inner voice, guide, and teacher—*you*—have become audible to yourself! This still may only come in the form of a whisper, but I assure you, the more you listen, the louder she becomes. You will begin to tap into and *feel* again, knowing that the

CONCLUSION

choices you are most aligned with are resonating from a place deep within you.

You will start to use your nervous system as your compass and, although you might not yet know how, it will unfold. You will begin to slowly trust saying no to the things that no longer feel good and yes to the ones that do, all the while leaning on the knowledge that you are not alone in this.

Being a cycle breaker means that you will pause and make a choice outside of and beyond old patterns, conditioning, and false beliefs. You will no longer do something because it's what you have always done. You will find other things that are aligned with being in your power and making a conscious choice. It means standing in your truth, even if you may no longer blend or even fit into the spaces that had once felt like home. You have outgrown them, and the knowledge that there is a new version of you—and women like her—on the other side will give you the security to keep going.

You are no longer clinging to known pain over unknown possibility. You are choosing alignment over approval, truth over tradition, and expanding over staying small. What once felt like home was built on a past version of you that wasn't truly you. But now, you are creating and building a new foundation, one rooted in wholeness, authenticity, and alignment.

You aren't leaving anyone behind, you are simply expanding beyond them. You aren't rejecting anyone or your past; you are simply growing into and embracing the fullest expression of you. Some will walk beside you and some may choose to stay where they are, and that's their choice. Your path is in honor of your evolution, and while you are on it you will learn to make space for those who align with you and are headed in the same direction. One step at a time, one choice, one decision. Each one leads you closer to the life you came here to live.

You need not see the whole path or have everything figured out. The only requirement is to take as many of your steps as possible from an aligned place, the place you've learned to identify by connecting with your body, heart, and soul. The place where you listen to your inner truth, not the *shoulds*, and choose to respond rather than react, honoring what matters most to you. The place where you pause, check in by asking yourself what you need in that moment, then wait for the answer. And because you are asking your whole self, the answer you receive will come from a place of clarity rather than fear.

With every step the path unfolds. With each decision you make, each bond you form with your whole self, the way forward becomes more clear. You are not lost—although at times it may feel unsteady. You are simply carving a path that hasn't yet been fully paved. You're on the road less traveled, the one that actually works for women, rather than asking women to work for others.

We're walking this path together, and our journey isn't about a fixed destination; it's a process of learning to trust ourselves, to lean on one another, knowing that where you are is exactly where you're meant to be. Acting courageously is moving from your heart. It's living and leading from your deepest truth, guided by the love, wisdom, and authenticity that resides within you. And when you do, people will show up in your life to help you, and situations will occur that can only be signs from the universe that this is the way.

The strangest things will start to happen as synchronicities align. You'll think of someone and they'll call you; you'll need something and it will appear. I can't explain it, but I have experienced it and can tell you with authority that

CONCLUSION

when you're living in alignment, you will have the same experiences as the path unfolds before you. When we are willing to drop all the noise and static that prevents us from fully stepping into ourselves, we are rewarded for doing so.

Through this book you have acquired new tools, insights, and a new paradigm for thinking. You have started to tune in and listen to your whole self. You have begun consciously parenting your ego, creating space for alignment and self-connection instead of forcing your way through life the way you have always done. These steps may seem small at first, but they are transformative. They are revolutionary—and so are you. You are co-creating a movement.

Every time you move from alignment, you are rewriting your story and the story of every little girl watching you. You are ensuring that the women of tomorrow will not silently suffer while daydreaming of the life they desire. You are carving the path for them to have more ease, joy, and freedom. You are showing them that having it all is less about your to-dos and more about who and how you be. You aren't teaching them this with your words, but you are powerfully instilling it into their subconscious programming by allowing them to witness your actions.

Every time you pause instead of react, you are shifting generational patterns. You are saying *this ends here, now, with me*.

Every time you embrace your whole self and make decisions that work for you in concert with your ego, you are showing the next generation how good this life can be. And when women come together and live our lives from this lens, we don't just change our own lives.

We change the world.

YOUR NEXT STEP

Right now, right here, is a community of women just like you. Women doing this for the first time. Women standing in their power, changing the narrative for all who come after. She is the fire that consumes old stories, burning away generations of conditioning, not to destroy but to clear space for something truer, freer, and more alive. She stands at the threshold like a mountain at sunrise, casting long shadows over the past but facing forward, golden and unshaken. She is the one who, with steady breath and an open heart, steps beyond the well-worn path to find a new one, blazing a trail for others to follow. Together, we can find alignment, listen to ourselves, break cycles, and support one another as we strive toward societal change.

This is your invitation.

Join us in this space as we walk this new path together. Join a community where you are seen, supported, and encouraged to keep courageously showing up for yourself. A community where you belong while becoming the truest, most whole version of yourself. Alignment isn't something we aim for once and check off our long to-do list. It's a way of being. It's a decision we make again and again. Over time it simply becomes who we are. And this journey is much more powerful when we embark on it together.

It's your time; it's your turn.

If you have been waiting for a sign, this is it.

Your greatest gift, your best guide, and most loyal companion has been with you all along. She was there with you in the quiet moments, whispering beneath all the noise. She was there in every gut feeling you have felt, even the ones you often ignored. She was with you when the sparks of inner truth sprang to life. She knew that you silenced every longing you have ever had, burying them beneath the pile

CONCLUSION

of *shoulds* and expectations. She has never left your side and never will. Anytime you have ever felt alone has merely been a result of you being taught to look everywhere but within.

But now, you remember.

You are not lost. You were never and will never be abandoned. You have never been *too much* or *not enough*. You have always fully belonged to yourself, to the moment in front of you, to the deep well of wisdom within your body that has been waiting for you to return.

This is your reunion.

This is your homecoming.

The connection that changes everything.

As you walk out onto the new path, know this—you are stepping into and onto something more expansive than yourself. You are walking on a path carved by every woman who finally dared to choose herself. And as you do so, you are leaving a light on for those who will come after you. So step forward, boldly, courageously, trusting that when you take the first step, the next one will appear.

Because the Connection Code was never something outside of you.

It was you, all along.

RESOURCES

The Connection Code (mentioned on page 101):
drmelissasonners.com/resources/connection-code

Sit Spot (mentioned on page 131):
Link to Video: You Need a Sit Spot Like This:
youtu.be/w7biHnjVFdk?si=IsNeVuHYHVFgSqiO

Roadmap to Realignment (mentioned on page 199):
drmelissasonners.com/resources/

My favorite tools for Sit Spot: drmelissasonners.com/red-light-guide

Stay up to date with all of Dr. Melissa's Tools & Resources to help keep you CONNECTED: drmelissasonners.com

ENDNOTES

Chapter 1

1. Joe Dispenza, *Breaking the Habit of Being Yourself: How to Lose Your Mind and Create a New One* (Carlsbad, CA: Hay House, Inc., 2013).

2. Michael Varnum, "Why and When Familiar Feels Good," *Psychology Today*, October 24, 2023. www.psychologytoday.com/us/blog/unserious-psychology/202310/why-and-when-the-familiar-feels-good.

3. Anna Lembke, *Dopamine Nation: Finding Balance in the Age of Indulgence* (New York: Dutton, 2021).

Chapter 3

4. Mita Mallick, "Moms Are Living in an Extraordinary Era of Burnout," Motherly, October 25, 2022. www.mother.ly/parenting/moms-suffering-from-pandemic-burnout/.

5. Christa Smith, "Working Moms Are Burned Out—It's Time for a Revolution," Accesswire, July 21, 2023. https://finance.yahoo.com/news/working-moms-burned-time-revolution-220500603.html; Maia Niguel Hoskin, "Moms Are Feeling More Anxious and Burned Out Than Ever, Even as the Pandemic Recedes," What to Expect, October 12, 2022. www.whattoexpect.com/news/first-year/survey-moms-feel-more-pressure-pandemic.

6. Smith, "Working Moms Are Burned Out—It's Time for a Revolution," July 21, 2023; "Have Working Moms Reached Their Breaking Point?," video, Fast Company, February 23, 2023. www.fastcompany.com/video/have-working-moms-reached-their-breaking-point/Kjmhqrhp.

7. Allie Volpe, "The Surprising Truth About Loneliness in America," Vox, August 13, 2024. www.vox.com/even-better/366620/loneliness-epidemic-coping-demographics-america-social-connection-mental-health.

Chapter 5

8. Frank Graff, "How Many Decisions Do We Make in One Day?," PBS North Carolina, last modified June 6, 2025. www.pbsnc.org/blogs/science/how-many-decisions-do-we-make-in-one-day/.

Chapter 8

9. Steve Bradt, "Wandering Mind Not a Happy Mind," *Harvard Gazette*, November 11, 2010. https://news.harvard.edu/gazette/story/2010/11/wandering-mind-not-a-happy-mind/.

Chapter 9

10. "New APA Poll: One in Three Americans Feels Lonely Every Week," American Psychiatric Association, news release, January 30, 2024. www.psychiatry.org/news-room/news-releases/new-apa-poll-one-in-three-americans-feels-lonely-e.

11. Daniel Cox, "The State of American Friendship: Change, Challenges, and Loss," Survey Center on American Life, June 8, 2021. www.americansurveycenter.org/research/the-state-of-american-friendship-change-challenges-and-loss/.

12. Bureau of Labor Statistics, "American Time Use Survey—2021 Results," U.S. Department of Labor, news release, June 23, 2021. www.bls.gov/news.release/archives/atus_06232022.pdf.

ACKNOWLEDGMENTS

This book came through me only after I reconnected with my whole self, and I truly believe that is the greatest gift we can ever give ourselves. And while the process can be simple, it is not always easy.

It asks you to stand up for boundaries you've never had before.

It asks you to listen to your nervous system and your intuition, even when the "yes" you think you should say is actually a crystal-clear no.

It asks you to have the courage to disappoint others so that you finally stop disappointing yourself.

It asks you to let friendships shift, relationships evolve, and old versions of you fall away.

So first, I need to thank myself.

For having the awareness to know this work mattered.

For realizing that I was worth the work.

For choosing alignment over approval, truth over comfort, and wholeness over performing.

And with that, I need to thank my husband.

It takes a true man to stand steady as a woman remembers who she came here to be. That journey can stir up insecurities, surface old wounds, and challenge every pattern in a relationship and yet you met me with presence, patience, and the kind of communication that makes us unstoppable.

Thank you for being one of the steadiest forces in my life.

I love this version of me not just for me, but for us.

Also, this process of stepping into who we came here to be is both a beautiful unfolding and one of the most vulnerable experiences I've ever walked through. I love the quote, "The funny thing about bravery is that when you're doing it right, it feels like fear."

This year has been one of the biggest seasons of growth and acceleration of my life. A year of sitting inside dreams I once wished for and then continuing to choose to show up as the woman those dreams require. With that comes imposter syndrome, the quiet question of *"Am I good enough?"* and so many other tender edges.

So I had to lean heavily on my community.

To the women who walked this path before me—thank you for reminding me, over and over again, "Yes, you're doing it right. These feelings are the price of admission. Keep going . . . here's how."

To my girl, Dr. Mindy Pelz, thank you for shining a light on my path. I watched you carve yours, and now you've stood beside me as I step fully into mine. Thank you for reflecting back what I'm capable of, for championing the version of me you always saw long before I did, and for holding space for the moments that felt hard and holy. I am forever grateful for our Voxer threads and everything unspoken inside them.

Dr. Sonya Jensen—my sister in authorship. You somehow always know exactly what to say, and always in the most beautifully poetic way. I've loved sharing this journey with you, two women writing truth into the world with our babies beside us. There's something sacred about that.

Ben Azadi—not just my friend, but my neighbor. Somehow, no matter what you have going on, you always make space for me. You lead with gratitude, you show up with generosity, and you've been a steady guide as I step deeper into my calling. It's been an honor watching you rise. Thank you for helping me rise too.

Dr. Mariza Snyder—my fellow lover of books. Love that I met you on this path and so excited to continue to be on this journey with you.

Thank you to all the incredible authors and people I admire who endorsed this book. Your support is palpable and so appreciated.

My girls—Melanie Hunter and Siobhan Lee. I often say that when we reconnect to our whole selves, our village finds us. You are living proof of that for me, the gift I received for finally being true to myself. You've made me a total girls' girl, and I am forever grateful to have found this kind of friendship at this stage of life.

ACKNOWLEDGMENTS

Thank you for being by my side this year, for being my village, and for stepping in with the kids anytime I needed support. I don't take it for granted for a second.

Thank you to other members of my village: Aleks Malkin, Melanie Duncan, Erin Kessous, Sabrina Ruz, and Michelle Kawas.

Aubry Marie—my little monkey-play buddy. Our Muscle Beach dates have been medicine this year. The sun, the sand, the monkey bars, they helped me drop back into my heart and refill my creative well.

And to you—the reader. Thank you for being here. Thank you for saying yes to yourself.

Every time you choose alignment over old patterns . . .

every time you choose truth over people-pleasing . . .

every time you choose connection instead of the numbing you once relied on . . .

you are breaking cycles that began long before you and would have continued long after you.

You may not always see it in the moment, but your yes to yourself is also a no.

A no to the resentment you inherited,

a no to the anger you were taught to swallow,

a no to the patterns that kept generations of women small, silent, or stretched thin.

When you choose differently, you live differently.

And when you live differently, everyone around you feels that shift.

Your children.

Your friends.

Your partner.

Your community.

And every future version of your lineage that will never have to unlearn what you've healed.

This is how the world changes. Not all at once, but one regulated, aligned, courageous woman at a time.

Your personal realignment becomes a public ripple. Your healing becomes a legacy.

Thank you for doing this work.

Thank you for returning to the woman you came here to be. The one who was always within you.

Thank you for walking this path with me . . . and for helping weave this movement into the lives of the women who walk beside you.

This is how we create our village again.

How we turn isolation into connection.

And how we remember that none of us were ever meant to do this alone.

To my parents, Roxi and Rick Murtaugh.

I am forever grateful for the way you raised me. The trust you helped me build in myself from such a young age by supporting me as I followed my heart, no matter how unconventional it looked, has shaped every part of who I am. You helped me form a deep connection with myself, with my inner guide, and you always encouraged me to boldly be led by my dreams. This book wouldn't have come through me without that foundation. Thank you.

To my brother Chad and my sister-in-law Selena. Thank you for always being there for comic relief whether through FaceTimes, the endless stream of funny reels, or when we're all together in person. With everything I'm leading and holding in my life, it's such a gift to slip back into being the little sister from time to time.

To my in-laws, Cheryl and Barry Sonners.

One of my favorite parts of marriage is expanding your family. Sitting around the table with you, diving into the "how" and the "why," and seeing the analytical lens that shaped Jason, even if it's not my usual way to play, has helped solidify my belief in myself. Thank you for welcoming me so fully into your world.

Thank you to my incredible Hay House team. Being part of the Hay House family is a full-circle moment. I grew up sitting on bookstore floors, finding Hay House books in seasons when I felt lost and needed a lighthouse. To now stand among the authors who once held me feels like pure magic, the kind that becomes possible when we finally live from our whole selves.

Patty Gift—I'll forever remember our meet-up in Arizona where I first shared the spark of this book. Your eyes lit up, and in that moment *The Connection Code* was born. I know this is only the beginning, and I'm so excited for all that's ahead.

Reid Tracy—I still have the voicemail you left me telling me I got the contract for this book and it remains one of my favorite

ACKNOWLEDGMENTS

messages I've ever received. I'm looking forward to getting more connected as we continue this journey together.

Sally Mason-Swaab—my incredible editor and true book midwife.

Your calm, loving, supportive presence held the safest container for me to speak my truth and share this message with the world. You guided me with such care and clarity, always helping me stay connected to the heart of what I wanted to say. I couldn't have imagined a more aligned partner in this process.

Tricia Breidenthal—my cover design magician.

I know this concept was a little out-of-the-box, and I'm so deeply grateful for how you listened, not just to my words, but to the feeling of the vision. You captured the fun, the playfulness, the lightness, the courage and all the energy I wanted reflected. I actually hope people judge this book by its cover. You absolutely nailed it. Thank you for helping me bring more sparkle and fun to the self-help section of the bookstore.

Marley Lynn. Thank you for workshopping these pages with me so intentionally and so artfully. Together we crafted something honest, meaningful, and deeply aligned. I'm proud of the rhythm we found and the story we told.

Thank you to my incredible behind-the-scenes team: Amanda, Luis, Cameron, and Christina for keeping everything moving with so much steadiness and heart.

And to my amazing Executive Assistant, Jirah DuPaul—thank you for holding down the fort and orchestrating every detail required to run this entire operation. I could not have stayed in alignment or played in the liminal space of the unknown this year without you.

Thank you for honoring that we were doing this my way and for always steering our ship toward what felt true in my heart, even when it wasn't the path of least resistance. Your support made this whole magic-carpet-ride year possible.

Thank you to our incredible team at Core Therapies and HBOT USA. These businesses were where I first learned how to dream, build, and lead and because of your steadiness, I was able to step back, listen inward, and fully step into the work I was meant to do next.

And finally, gratitude for my friend and one of my greatest guides, Annie Yatch.

The work we did together was a true MACRO immersion, a powerful reconnection with my little girl Missy Mouse, the red-cheeked kiddo who rode her bike with a doll strapped to her chest, daydreaming and feeling completely free. I am forever grateful for that experience.

Thank you for helping me remember her and fiercely protect her by asking multiple times daily what she would want in this moment and doing that. Thank you for reminding me that this work isn't a onetime breakthrough but a daily devotion—a thousand micro connections that rebuild trust, safety, and self-love. She and I together are unstoppable. And so is every woman who bridges the gap between who she truly is and who the world once told her to be.

And the truth is, it doesn't have to be complicated. This version of us already knows what she wants and needs. We just have to start asking her more, inviting her into the conversation, and taking the one small step she's guiding us toward, the one that feels fun, alive, light-you-up-from-the-inside true.

Because when we re-embrace this relationship, the one with our own inner girl, life becomes more whole, more fun, more free.

And that is the heart of all of this.

That is how we live the Connection Code. By coming home to ourselves, one small, wholehearted connection at a time.

ABOUT THE AUTHOR

Dr. Melissa Sonners is a nervous-system guide, brainwave educator, and global speaker leading a movement to rebrand self-care from something you do to something you feel. She helps women shift out of survival mode and back into the most grounded, playful, lit-up version of themselves.

After losing herself somewhere between motherhood and ambition, Dr. Melissa realized that chronic illness forced her to rebuild from the inside out. She discovered that healing wasn't about doing more—it was about listening more deeply.

Now she teaches simple two-minute tools, rhythm syncing, and brainwave practices that bring more calm, more clarity, and a whole lot more joy into everyday life. Her work helps people remember the version of themselves who laughs easier, breathes deeper, and feels fully alive.

She lives in Miami with her family, where she believes sunshine, a long bike ride, and a two-minute lizard-gazing brain break can heal almost anything.

Website: **drmelissasonners.com**

CONNECT WITH
HAY HOUSE
ONLINE

🌐 hayhouse.co.uk   **f** @hayhouse

📷 @hayhouseuk   🦋 @hayhouseuk.bsky.social

♪ @hayhouseuk   ▶ @HayHousePresents

Find out all about our latest books & card decks • Be the first to know about exclusive discounts • Interact with our authors in live broadcasts • Celebrate the cycle of the seasons with us • Watch free videos from your favourite authors • Connect with like-minded souls

'The gateways to wisdom and knowledge are always open.'

Louise Hay